D1452529

The
Price
of
Truth:

A true story of child sexual abuse in the
Orthodox Jewish world --
and one girl's courage to survive.

Genendy

Lioness

I was going to die
If not sooner than later
Whether or not I'd ever spoken myself
My silence did not protect me.
Your silence will not protect you.
Audre Lorde

Contents

Dedication

This book is dedicated to my incredible husband, my dear friend, life partner and soulmate. Your commitment to truth and personal growth inspires me every day. You bring an abundance of joy and love to my life. I am so blessed!

I also dedicate this book to my three amazing children. Each of you is a unique gem in a priceless setting. I love you more than words can express. It is an honor and privilege to be your mother.

Note to my siblings and relatives:

I have always done my best to tell the truth, and I will continue to do so. Unfortunately, I did not have any family members to check the narrative of our family history with. I have written it to the best of my ability as I remember it being told to me as a child, in anecdotes and stories from our parents. If I have erred in relating a historical fact, I ask your forgiveness in advance.

This is a memoir of my subjective memories, experiences and reactions to my childhood. Your memories, experiences and reactions may be very different from my own, and that is valid. If your memories are less painful than mine, I am truly happy for you.

I believe that as a family we can heal. I believe that those of us who are committed to truth will find a meeting of hearts in the very near future in joy, understanding and peace.

Love,
Genendy

Acknowledgements

I thank you My Creator, the Source of all life and love, for giving me the opportunity to make a positive difference in Your world, and for sending me perfect messengers in each moment of my journey to help me survive the unbearable, heal and thrive, and make this project a reality.

Thank you Dr. Elana Sztokman, my editor, publisher and friend. I am so grateful to you for enabling me to share my story with so many, for sharing my vision and encouraging and supporting me in the process, and for helping me to write so clearly and beautifully.

Thank you to Tzippora Price, my first editor and writing mentor. You shared my vision and helped me see what was missing and what was needed, and pointed me in the right direction.

Thank you to Hadas Boxer, and Chava and Shaul Bloom, for reading the manuscript and giving me invaluable feedback.

Thank you to my wonderful and dedicated therapist Deena Mendlowitz. What a journey we have been on together! I love you very much.

Thank you to therapist Juliet Mandelzwig who helped me to re-learn touch.

Thank you to therapists Rachel Ackerman and Joan Krystal, and of course my irreplaceable group. Thank you for your courage and friendship.

Thank you to Shana Aronson and Meyer Seewald of JCW. Two remarkable human beings who have dedicated their lives to ridding our community of the evil of child sexual abuse. You have made a huge difference to myself and so many countless survivors.

Thank you to my wonderful parents-in-law Mom and Dad R. and my brother-in-law M. and partner S. for all of your love and support. You are my family!

There are so many exceptional people who without your love and support I would not be here today, and this book would not exist. To name just a few more that come to mind in this moment:

Hinda and Yosef G., Ruth and Simcha Frischling, Brian Miller, Ilana Miller, Yarden Frankl, and Stella Frankl, (of blessed memory) Rabbi, and Sara Blooming, Rabbi Krimsky, and Amy Federman.

The lifesaving staff at the trauma disorders day hospital and the compassionate and caring staff at the Elizabeth House, Elizabeth, Debra, Terry, Joan, Susan, Deborah, and Dr. F.

Therapists Victor Welzant, Dr. Donna Small, and Dr. John Gershefsky, who guided me through engagement, marriage, and childbirth.

Lisa and Shlomo Zalman Jessel, Hadas and Yaakov Boxer, Eva and Ari Soller, Yedudah Buchwalter, Atara and Rabbi Hillel Waxman, Chana Ginzberg, Nechami P. Orit Riter, Miriam Segal, Andrea Kornfeld, Donna Abraham, Susie Zettel, Yael Soussan, Chaya Bluma Gadenyan, Dr. Miriam Adahan, Rabbi Yosef Blau, Yehudah and Yocheved S. Frady, Evelyn Shnier, Miriam R., Yaakov S., Rena and Yisroel S., Blimi and Menachem S., Bicki V., Dalit Kimor, and my and my Magen buddies, …I don't know if you realize how critical you were to my healing process, David Morris, who inspired the name of this book , Hillel Abrahams, Miriam Freedman, Batya Cohen, and Helise Pollak.

Thank you for being you!!

If I have failed to mention your name, please accept my apologies, and know that I thank you with all of my heart!

*All names in this book have been changed except
for my own first name, Dr. Miriam Adahan, Rabbi Aaron Kotler and
Rabbi Shlomo Zalman Urbach
(of blessed memory).*

OPENING SCENES

The Princess Story

"Mommy, tell me the story about the princess, and the king who did something bad to her."

My four-and-a-half-year-old daughter jumps into my lap, her glittery purple princess crown sliding down over her eyes.

"Oh, Avital, it's Friday. I shouldn't be sitting here. I still have to get the guest room ready, and I really have to be in the right headspace to tell you that story."

"Oh, please, please tell it to me Mommy. PLEASE!"

My beautiful princess gazes into my tired eyes, hers filled with trust and anticipation.

She doesn't know that the story I am about to tell her is true. It's a story that happened to me, and to many other Jewish girls, princesses, all of us.

It's a story I need her to know for her own safety. I guess I can stand to take a break.

Avital and I settle into our comfy blue leather couch.

"Once upon a time there was a beautiful little princess," I begin. "She lived in a palace with her father the king and her mother the queen. She had sisters who were also princesses and brothers who were princes. The princess was a good girl and a kind girl. She cared about others' feelings. She went to school every day and had a teacher who loved her, and who she loved."

"Now the princess had a big problem and she didn't know what to do," I continue. "Maybe you and I can help her find a good solution."

"Her father the king sometimes did things to her and the other princesses that she knew were not okay. Things that a king shouldn't do and usually doesn't do."

"What did he do Mommy?"

"He did things that were not *tzanuah* (modest). He touched the princesses in private places."

"A king wouldn't do that Mommy!"

"That's exactly what the queen said when the princess told her. She said, 'The king would never do such a thing!'"

"The princess didn't know what to do. She loved the king and didn't want to hurt his feelings. But she wanted him to stop touching her. She tried to tell her sisters but they wouldn't listen to her either. The princess believed that her sisters knew the truth but they were too embarrassed and ashamed to admit it. What should the princess do to help herself and her family? Should she keep it a secret? Who should she tell?"

Avital knows the answer.

How can she not? I'm her mother.

"She should tell. Even if she's embarrassed, she should tell!"

"Well, that is just what the princess did. Her teacher hugged her and said, 'I am so proud of you for telling me. You are a very brave girl!'"

"But then the teacher turned serious. 'Is the king doing these things to anyone else?'"

"'Yes,' the princess said. 'To my sisters. To my friends. And to my brother, the prince.' Guess what the teacher said?"

Avital knows this answer as well.

"She has to tell!"

"Yes. You are so smart. As smart as the princess in the story. The teacher indeed said, 'You have to tell. You have to yell from the roof of the castle until people listen and stop him.'"

"The princess shook her head. 'But I'm embarrassed,' she said. 'And the king and the queen won't let me live in the palace anymore if I tell everyone. They will be so angry with me. They will say it's not true! Where will I live?'"

"The teacher gazed firmly and lovingly into the princess's eyes. 'If that happens then you will live with me. I will love you and take care of you for ever and ever.'"

"Well, that is exactly what happened. The princess yelled from the rooftop of the palace about the king and his terrible touching problem. The king and the queen were very angry and embarrassed, and insisted that it wasn't true. They commanded that the princess leave the castle. Many people in the kingdom were upset. They thought the princess must be wrong. They said, 'The king would never do such a thing!'"

"The princess was sad and scared but she knew just what to do. She went to her teacher who loved her, believed her, and protected her. The teacher made a big party to celebrate the princess's bravery and invited all of her friends from school. She made her a special dress and crown that was befitting such a brave and courageous princess."

For my four-year-old princess this happens to be the most important part of the story.

"Tell me more about the dress and crown that she wore at the party!" she begs me.

"Her dress was splendid," I respond. "It was white with gold threads, and real diamonds and pearls woven into it. Pink glittery gauze covered the whole thing. The dress sparkled in the light. When the princess spun around her dress twirled and swirled with her. Her crown was made out of gold and was engraved with the words: *'A Real Princess Inside and Out'*."

Now comes the million-dollar question. Deep breath.

"If you were the princess," I ask, "do you think you would tell, like she did?"

"*Of course* I would!"

Sigh.

I sure hope so.

Loss

Many years ago, I lost my parents, 11 siblings and countless relatives. Today, I don't know who in my family is alive or dead, who is married, who has children.

No, I am not a Holocaust survivor. I am an incest survivor, from a family of Torah scholars. But I did not keep it a secret, as I was told to. As a result, I have been excommunicated.

I was not invited to my siblings' weddings. I have tens of nieces and nephews I have never met and wouldn't recognize on the street. Around Jewish holidays, which most of us spend with family, I feel orphaned.

I grew up *frum* – that is, in an ultra-Orthodox Jewish family. My maternal grandfather, my father, and other men in my grandfather's *yeshiva* (religious school) molested me when I was very young. I had no one to turn to at the time. As a teen and young adult, I never thought I would survive, marry or have children. Every day was a struggle. I believed that what happened to me was unusual. I thought I was the only one. I believed the only escape from the pain was suicide.

My determination, my faith, and my choices in dealing with my painful reality made the difference – literally – between life and death. Today, I am blessed to have been married for 20 years to a wonderful man. We have three beautiful children. I work as an educator, a writer, and a child safety activist.

I am, indeed, one of the lucky ones. Yet, my past still haunts me.

Incest, the most prevalent form of child sexual abuse, is still taboo. Its existence – even among the most Torah-observant families – is not discussed or acknowledged, nor is the impact that it has on a child, a family, and a community.

I remain part of the Orthodox Jewish community, living and working among them, and raising my children as Torah-observant Jews, despite communal efforts to silence me and to chase me away.

Perhaps I stayed in order to be able to tell my story. Maybe by speaking out in this way I can help save the community from its greatest weakness: our blinding need to protect our image.

Or perhaps I stayed because I recognize that child abuse exists in every community and there is no community that is safe.

Or perhaps I stayed for more personal reasons. Maybe I chose not only to stay alive, but also to live a Torah life because I already lost enough, and I will not allow anyone to rob me of my beautiful heritage as well.

Ironically, it is because of my family's inability to hear me that I must expose my pain to the world. I exist in spite of their attempts to make me and my memories disappear.

As strange as this may sound, I understand why my family wants me silenced. They need to hold on to their image of the "normal" family. It is so much harder and more painful to deal with the reality. I truly believe that they may not be capable of dealing with the reality. I did not think I was capable. I realize now that I was given a gift of strength that perhaps my siblings do not have.

I believe that I have a role to play within my family, and within the Jewish nation. I see the Jewish nation as one body with many parts. We are all different. We are not meant to be the same. We have different makeups and different missions. I believe that we all need each other. I need my family and they need me, just as each one of us needs each other and is responsible for the whole. By focusing on our individual missions, we heal a part of the greater body of the Jewish nation, and the world. My personal mission is love, acceptance, and healing of my family and my community. I cannot cut them off just as I could not voluntarily cut off my own limb.

I am real, and my story is true, and it is time for my voice to be heard.

It takes tremendous risk and vulnerability to tell my story publicly. But I believe that my family and my community are worth the risk. My book is more than a personal journey of healing. It also carries a powerful message of hope for my community.

Incest touches almost every family in every community in the world. I hope that my story will sensitize you to the child or adult in your life who is crying out for help, no matter what community you come from.

Family origins

I was born in the United States, in 1973, the third of 12 children, and the third daughter of Rena and Gabe, who were almost 24 and 28 years old respectively when I was born.

My father's mother, Savta, came to the United States from Czechoslovakia at the age of 15. A rich uncle paid her ticket to America and to freedom from the horror at home in Europe. Savta's parents and siblings were not so lucky, and they perished in the Holocaust.

At four-foot-ten, Savta was a powerhouse of energy, motion, and emotion. She ran her life with order and rules, perhaps with a need to control what little she could in her life. My grandparents' two-bedroom apartment in Boro Park was always uncomfortably neat and organized. The wall-to-wall green carpeting was cleaned with a hand-held carpet sweeper minutes after a crumb fell. The living room couch was covered in thick plastic to keep it pristine, which stuck to the back of my legs when I tried to stand up. A plastic tree with two small plastic birds perched on it – and not a speck of dust – stood in one corner of the living room. A covered glass dish of sucking candies sat on a small round table between two easy chairs in front of the window where Savta would sometimes open the blinds and yell out to the Super's kids to go get their father if she needed something. Everything had its place at Savta's and it had to stay there. Nothing could be moved or touched without permission and a good reason.

The square, empty, high-ceilinged lobby at the entrance to her building had a wonderful echo. We couldn't resist testing it out every time we walked into her building, to the chagrin of my parents and Savta who tried, often unsuccessfully, to keep us quiet. Savta lived on the ground floor, which prevented us from having to use the tiny elevator that closed with a lever and bumped and jerked its way up and down the shaft. Our hair and clothes had to be just so when we arrived, and Savta would grab each of us close and kiss us hard, and she expected a strong kiss back.

Those who resisted – like my younger sister, Chaya, who would wipe her cheek, refuse to return the kiss, and say, "Icky kisses!" – were mocked, and fell out of favor with Savta.

There were pictures of us, the grandchildren, displayed everywhere. We were her prize trophies, especially in photos, where we didn't move around too much, make any messes or do anything to offend her. Savta's apartment smelled of potato kugel, homemade gefilte fish and fricassee. Savta took pride in feeding us her homemade dishes, especially her famous kukush cake and potato kugel, which had to come out flawlessly white every time or get thrown in the trash. Savta always took us shopping for clothes and shoes, to visit her friends, and to *shul* (synagogue) with her on *Shabbos* (the Sabbath). She showed us off to anyone she could. "These are my grandchildren!" she would say with pride, rolling her r.

Grandpa, born and raised in New York City, had a disposition that was the antithesis of Savta's storm. He was as even-tempered as she was moody, calm as she was anxious. The slight, clean-shaven man of 5'7" spoke in a quiet, soothing voice. I can still hear Savta's yells as she discovered that someone once again put their shoes in the wrong spot or forgot to hang a jacket, followed by Grandpa's low, soothing voice.

Grandpa had been a furrier before the big stock market crash. He earned the name "Honest Joe" when, after losing everything in the crash, he paid back every debt that he owed to the last penny. Grandpa consistently asked us how we were doing, how school was going, and what we were learning. I always answered politely but with reservation, and I never felt that I knew Grandpa very well, or that he knew me at all.

My father, the middle child of three siblings, had a sister one year older and a head shorter than him, and a brother who was two years younger. At six feet tall, with an athletic build, Tatty was a trained lifeguard who had once saved a boy from drowning. As a teen, he was a star on the basketball court, sometimes playing six hours a day.

Tatty's dark skin and hair, and prominent ears and nose, were stereotypically Jewish, although his surprisingly light eyes were a hazel mix of light browns and greens. He spoke with a calm, gentle voice, much like his father.

My mother's father, Zaidy, came from Europe with the famous Rabbi Aaron Kotler when the rabbi moved his *yeshiva* from Ponovez to Lakewood New Jersey in 1943. Zaidy was a protégé of Rav Aaron, as he was known, a brilliant student known to understand Rav Aaron's esoteric *shiurim* (lessons) in a way that not many did. Zaidy was the youngest of three children and was known as a *talmid chacham* (brilliant student) and an up and coming *gadol hador* (a great man of the generation) from a young age. Zaidy married the daughter of a famous *dayan* (religious judge) from England who had escaped the Holocaust by dressing up as a woman. Zaidy loved her dearly. Together they made a home near the *yeshiva*, but soon left for the open countryside where Zaidy opened his own *yeshiva*.

Zaidy did not want to offer competition to Rav Aaron by opening another *yeshiva* close by. So, he bought an old motel off a main road in the middle of nowhere and converted half of it into a house for his rapidly growing family, and the other half into a *bais medrish* (religious house of study), which included a *yeshiva* dining room, kitchen and dorm rooms. The sprawling, three-storey, white motel came with ample real estate, including a field that later was rented out to grow soybeans. The land around the *yeshiva* was green with tall, calming trees. In the front of the family's side door was an unpaved circular drive ending in an area for three or four cars to park.

To the right of the driveway was a stone shed where two cows had once lived. Along the west side of the property were chicken coops and goat sheds, which Zaidy's son, my uncle Moishe, cared for. The chickens provided fresh eggs, and the cows and goats provided fresh milk. To the left of the screened front porch, which was used more as a side door, was a tall iron swing set, which my aunts and uncles regularly used as children. To the far right was a basketball court, and a bit further on, a road. On the other side of the road was a lake, where Tatty and his friends would sometimes fish.

Zaidy was a charismatic and strict leader and teacher, expecting his hand-picked students to maintain a high level of learning and modesty. He taught a daily *"mussar"* *shiur* (class in "morals"). The students were not allowed into the *bais medrish* in short sleeves, and during the hot summer heat they would wrap napkins around their elbows instead of changing into long-sleeve shirts. Zaidy had many *chumros* (strict additions) to *halakha* (religious law), and was himself a strict adherent of *halakha*. My mother knew, for example, that if she accidentally tied her shoelace in a knot on Friday night, she would end up sleeping with the shoe on because untying knots on *Shabbos* was prohibited. Modesty was also interpreted in the strictest ways. My mother and her sisters always wore their long hair in two long braids, for example, as loose hair was considered immodest. Zaidy's *yeshiva* developed a reputation as elite, selective and exclusive.

Tatty internalized the idea that he was lucky to get into Zaidy's *yeshiva*, and that it was not because of his own merit as a student of Torah learning, and that it must have been divine providence. After bouncing from one *yeshiva* to another and having been kicked out of more than one institution, he finally landed on Zaidy's doorstep at the age of 18. Tatty begged Zaidy to take him in, promising to work hard and succeed in learning. Tatty sensed that this was his last chance at living the life he dreamed of and he begged Zaidy to give him a chance. He felt his life depended on getting into Zaidy's *yeshiva*.

Perhaps Zaidy felt sorry for him when, during an impassioned discussion, Zaidy raised his arm with vigor and Tatty quickly ducked under the table to avoid what he thought was an imminent slap. Tatty explained that Savta would regularly beat him. Perhaps Zaidy saw Tatty's potential or maybe his desperate need. In any case, he allowed Tatty to stay, and Tatty did not disappoint. Tatty told me later that Zaidy had pulled him from the garbage.

My mother was the oldest of ten children and only 15 years old when tragedy struck, forever changing my family's history. My young grandmother, Zaidy's wife, suddenly became ill with a molar pregnancy. Complications developed. Three months later she was dead at the age of 36, leaving Zaidy with ten young children and a *yeshiva* full of students to care for.

Zaidy sent all of the *bochurim,* (pronounced BUḤ-rim – young men studying in *yehiva*) away, including Tatty, and closed himself and his children inside the house. He would not let anyone in or out. His wife's family in England, far away and busy with their own growing families, wanted to help, but for some reason were not welcome. My mother hinted that there was friction between her mother's family and Zaidy. Eventually, a friend finally convinced Zaidy to let him into the house and helped him slowly get back on his feet.

To help heal from their huge loss, my mother, aunts and uncles were each given an instrument and music lessons. Zaidy re-opened the *yeshiva*, although he was a shadow of his former self. A few *bochurim* returned to the *yeshiva*, including Tatty. From then on, the *yeshiva* stayed very small, and it would never be the same.

Zaidy's office was off the family dining room, and Tatty would regularly walk through the house to speak with him in his office. He and other students were often invited to join the family for *Shabbos* meals. Tatty was smitten by my gentle, slim, blue-eyed, dark-haired mother, and decided that he wanted to marry her. He also knew that if he married my mother he would not only have a beautiful, modest and gentle wife but would also become part of Zaidy's family, part of the *yichus* (rabbinic lineage).

Tatty wrote a heartfelt letter to Zaidy asking him for permission to marry my mother. Zaidy finally agreed that they could meet, and that my mother would decide. They met in the family dining room for 15 minutes. Tatty told my mother everything that he thought was wrong with him. Then he proposed, saying, "This is my life's work. Will you share it with me?" My mother said yes.

She would have said yes to anyone, desperate as she was to get out of the house under Zaidy's strict discipline and occasional violence. My mother told me that her brothers would try to protect her from Zaidy's angry hand, especially since after her mother died, his rage was often directed at her. My mother had been a substitute mother to nine children for three years when Tatty proposed. She thought this tall, dark young man with the gentle voice was handsome. And she also knew that Zaidy liked Tatty and approved of the *shidduch* (set-up for an arranged marriage).

My parents were married in a rented circus tent on the *yeshiva* lawn. My mother was 19 years old and Tatty was 23. Relatives came from all over the world. Savta insisted that my mother call her "Mommy" as she didn't have a mother of her own, and my mother complied.

I always knew that we were very lucky to be *frum* (observant Jews). We had Torah and *mitzvos* (commandments) which dictated exactly how to live every aspect of our lives. We were Litvish from Lithuanian descent, not Hassidic. Lithuanians consider themselves elite and more serious. Hassidic Jews, who followed the Ba'al Shem Tov in the early 19th century as he made Torah and divine connection available to the masses in the European *shtetls*, (small Jewish towns or villages) were considered lesser in the eyes of the Lithuanians.

In our family lore, we knew this hierarchy well. My mother would say that Hassidism was more about dress and not about Torah learning. It was about emotion and joy rather than about serious Torah study. Becoming a Torah scholar was everything to my family. My mother explained to me that today Hassidim learn more Torah and the Litvish learn less Torah, so the difference is in large part in the dress. In fact, it was not unheard of for a Litvish family to sit *shiva* (mourn) for a child who became a Hassid. This is the world that Zaidy inhabited.

My mother and her brothers and sisters attended a small co-ed Jewish day school until the fourth grade. After that age, Zaidy did not consider mixed education an option. Anyway, by the time I was born, the school was long gone.

My oldest sister Gittel was born a year after my parents' wedding and was followed two and a half years later by my sister Hadassa. I was born exactly one year after Hadassa. I was told that I did not cry when I was born, but immediately stuck the two middle fingers of my left hand into my mouth and began to suck, looking around at my new surroundings with wide round blue eyes. (My eyes would turn brown after I was a year old.)

The first home I remember is a small white stucco house with a stone blue-gray front porch. We were a few minutes' drive from Zaidy's *yeshiva*. The front yard was small. The front door to our home opened into a living room with a brown carpet. There was no sofa in the living room, only a large overstuffed chair that was for Tatty and guests, not us kids. Directly behind the living room was a square hallway with five doorways leading off it. On the left were two bedrooms, with a bathroom in between. My parents used one bedroom and I shared the second one with my younger sister and baby brother. At the back of the hallway was the dining room, and behind the dining room a tiny kitchen, and a back door leading out to the yard and a swing set like the one in *yeshiva*. In the corner of the dining room was a staircase which led up to a finished attic, which had two rooms with slanted ceilings. Gittel and Hadassa shared one of the rooms and the other was used for storage.

Tatty often took care of us, as my mother was usually pregnant or caring for a newborn. He would take us to the beach, rowing on the lake or swimming in the pool at the local Holiday Inn. Sometimes, while Tatty learned, we were cared for by my doting teenage aunts and uncles who were more like older siblings to us.

There was a small Hebrew school class that had survived the closing of the Jewish day school. Tatty taught the class and Gittel was the only one old enough to attend. Few Jewish families lived in town, and many of those who did worked in the local kosher chicken slaughterhouse.

Tatty could be strict but could also be a lot of fun and played tickling and caressing games with us. He liked to sing us a Yiddish lullaby that he learned from Savta: "*Hi lee loo lee loo… Shluf, shluf, mine tiyere meidele…*" *Sleep, sleep my dear little girl.*

Tatty learned in *yeshiva* during the morning hours and my mother would announce excitedly when Tatty called her to tell us he was on his way home for lunch. My two older sisters and I would run to the living room and lie in a row, giggling, on the living room carpet to greet him. Tatty would lift our blouses and blow "poo!" on our bellies.

Gittel taught herself to read at the age of three. She would read the headlines and captions in the local newspaper and offer comment, much to my parents' surprise. Hadassa, exactly one year older than me, was also bright, but apparently of a very different temperament than me.

From a young age, Hadassa was often punished and was considered "wild." My mother called her a troublemaker. Although she was two and a half years younger than Gittel, she taught our older sister how to hit. I remember Tatty washing Hadassa's mouth out with soap after she spit at the non-Jewish neighbor boy. She was often angry with me and my sisters, instigating fights with us, hitting and calling us names. Maybe she was angry because my mother stopped nursing her at three months old when she became pregnant with me, feeding her instead bananas, which gave her a life-long aversion to the fruit. Looking back, I think that three-year-old Hadassa was acting out her anger and pain, while I was internalizing and dissociating mine.

Although Gittel was five years old and I was barely three, Gittel, Hadassa and I were Tatty's "three big girls," since we already had two younger siblings – Chaya, who was born two years after me and, much to my parents' surprise and delight, the first boy and grandson, my brother Tzvi, was born one year later. Having learned from her experience with Hadassa, my mother did not stop nursing Chaya when she became pregnant with my brother. Having so many siblings so close in age was hard on me. I did not feel like I could ever be truly alone and present with my mother. I was one in a crowd. My identity merged with those of my siblings.

PART 1:

SECRETS

The hole in my hand and other events

I recall thoughts and feelings that I had as a two-year-old as if I am living them right now.

I see something in the clothing store that I really want. It's a doll that's the size of a real live baby boy. He wears real clothes and real shoes. We can't buy him because he is a mannequin. That means he is not for sale.

I wish I could have that doll. I need that doll. I want to take him home. I want to take off his clothes. I want to hurt him and scare him. Then I will dress him again and hug him and help him feel better. I overhear Mommy telling Tatty that he gives in to me too much. She said he gives me whatever I want. I never noticed that he gives me whatever I want. He didn't give me that doll that I want.

I am lying in bed in a room that I share with my sister and brother in our little white stucco house.

I am two.

Tatty comes into my room and lies down on my bed.

I am too scared to move.

I know what will happen and I know it's because I'm a very bad girl.

I stare at the red and white checkered curtains.

I can't get away from him.

No, Tatty, No! Don't hurt me!

He rolls on top of me. I can't breathe. I can't move. Something is poking at me. I can't see what it is. It's cutting me. He's too heavy. I am going to die.

I want to die.

I have to die.

Something is in my mouth. I can't breathe.

Tatty, NO!

Tatty, I need you!

My eyes are staring into the dark inside my head. It feels floaty in here. I move away from my body and away from Tatty.

Away from everything.

I am not real.

I can't be…

I want to fly up to the sky. But not too high in the sky.

I don't want to be too close to Hashem [God].

I believe Hashem is probably like my Tatty and likes to touch and hurt little girls.

I don't want to go anywhere near Hashem.

I know that Hashem sees everything.

I don't know why He lets Tatty hurt me.

Maybe He likes to watch.

Maybe He knows that I deserve to be hurt.

I wonder if I could be dead and still stay far away from Hashem.

My throat hurts when I think about how Hashem lets me get hurt, and watches. I wish someone could make it better. Maybe magic will make the bad parts of me disappear and then Tatty won't hurt me anymore. I wish I was a different girl, then, maybe, I could be safe.

I want to fly to the clouds, in between the sky and Hashem, where there are no people.

I can crawl inside a fluffy cloud and feel safe for a few minutes. I don't have to be me up here. I can pretend I'm good and pretend I'm safe. No one can bother me or fight with me. No one can touch me or hurt me. I can turn into a cloud and float away.

Far, far away…

I wake up in the morning and I remember nothing.

Mommy fixes broken things. She fixes socks, and other things with holes, with a needle and a thread. Mommy put the sewing box in her dresser, and I need it.

I open the top drawer of Mommy's short white dresser. I can see my brown hair and red hairpin in the mirror behind it. My hair is brown and shiny, very thick and straight, like sticks. The rest of me is not visible in the mirror because I am too short. For a moment I panic. Where is the rest of me?

I look down and see my red shirt and brown pants. The rest of me is right here!

Soon, when I'm three, I'll be too big to wear pants and Mommy will put them away. I need my pants. I don't want Mommy to take them.

I feel around in the drawer because I can't see all the way inside. I feel clothing and a brush.

I know I am not supposed to take things from Mommy's drawer, but this is for a good reason.

I pull out a white brush with black prickles and rub my fingers over an orange flower on the handle. The flowers are rubbing off. I quickly put the brush down on top of the dresser.

Mommy doesn't want me to rub off her flowers. I stick my hand back in the drawer.

Here it is. I can feel its shape. The sewing box. I smell a funny smell on it. Mommy says it's mothballs. She puts mothballs in the drawers and in the closets with the clothes so the moths don't eat them. I never saw moths eating our clothes.

I put the box down on Mommy's big bed, with the blue bedspread and the white flowers.

A slide of light is coming from the window all the way down to Mommy's bed. Little dust pieces are dancing on the slide of light. I wave my hand through the dust and they run away from my hand. I clap and more dust comes. I can't feel the dust but I can see it, and I can make it dance.

My fingers are pushing at the clasp on the box, working hard. Now the box is open. I take out a pointed sewing needle. I hear Mommy's voice outside the door. I quickly open the fingers of one hand and grab the needle tight with my other hand.

I need to fix myself.

I push the needle into my hand near my thumb. It feels like nothing. When I can't push it in any more I try to pull the needle out. It won't move. I wiggle it around and, oh! I see red blood on my hand! I pull hard and… uh oh… the needle broke. A piece of it is stuck inside my hand.

I hear the doorknob and Mommy is here. She says, "Oy!" She takes my arm. She is telling me things. Telling me I did something wrong. I can feel her upset. She hurries me into the kitchen.

She wipes the blood off my hand. Mommy says we have to go to the emergency room and the doctor will sew stitches in my hand. I don't want the doctor to sew it; I want Mommy to fix it.

Please, Mommy, you sew it shut.

Sew shut all the bad holes in me.

The holes that are broken and bloody.

The holes that shouldn't be...

I need Mommy to see the other hole with the blood, the one that Tatty made.

I wish she could fix that hole too, with a needle and thread.

Mommy is not allowed into the white room with the funny smell, and the big lights, while the doctor is fixing my hand. She is watching from the door. She is so far away.

The table is so high. The room is so big. It smells funny. I am strapped down in a purple straightjacket. I am crying and the doctor tells me, "Shut your mouth!" I shut my mouth. I can cry with my mouth shut. When the nurse comes in I stop crying because I see something funny. It's the nurse's tiny hat.

I say, "The nurse's hat is too small!" When the hole in my hand is fixed, the nurse gives me a purple lollipop. Mommy says I can't eat it because it's not kosher. She will give me something else at home. I give the lolly to her, but I don't really want to.

Purple is my favorite flavor.

Yeshiva is where Zaidy lives, and where all the *tantas* (aunts) and uncles live. I love going there to play with my aunts and uncles and swing on the swing set. One time, before I was born, my uncle Baruch went so high on the swing that he swung over the bar, fell off and broke his arm. I am careful not to go that high.

My favorite uncle, Uncle Moishe, takes care of the animals. Sometimes I go with him to the chicken coop to look for eggs. The scent of chickens, the fresh straw, and the sound of clucking accompany us. We have goats in *yeshiva* too, and we used to have cows but the cows were fighting, so they had to get rid of them. That was before I was born.

We almost always go into *yeshiva* through the side door to the kitchen. I relax playing near the big tree with the leaves in front of the side door. Uncle Moishe is always happy to see me.

He swings me through his legs and up to the sky! I laugh. I like Uncle Moishe. He juggles three balls and can jump on a pogo stick with no hands. I am happy in *yeshiva* with my aunts and uncles during the day.

There are so many rooms in *yeshiva*. More than I have ever seen before.

The kitchen is big and rectangular. The stove is right near the door to the dining room. I am not supposed to touch it just in case it is hot. I often touch it quickly to check for myself.

I watch Tanta Yocheved preparing food for Zaidy on the kitchen table. I smell the fresh cantaloupe melon she is cutting. Zaidy comes in and Tanta Yocheved asks, "Does Deddy want Deddy's food yet?"

He says, "Soon."

He goes to the sink to wash his hands.

I wonder why Mommy, Tatty, and all the *tantas* and uncles talk to Zaidy like that. Like they are talking to a baby.

It is very important for everyone, including me, to do what Zaidy wants and to keep him from getting angry.

The *bochurim*

The floor in the dining room squeaks near the table, where I stop to look at the picture on the wall near Zaidy's office. Tanta Leah drew it when she was 13.

It is a picture of boys sitting at tables in a *bais medrish* learning Torah. There is a clock drawn on the wall in the picture. It is a special picture because the boys are learning Torah, and learning Torah, I know, is the most important thing in the world.

I walk through the door to the *yeshiva* side of the house, and pass the stairs going up to the bedrooms of the *bochurim,* on the second floor. I pass the *bochurim*'s bathrooms and kitchen.

I try not to use those bathrooms unless I really can't wait.

Sometimes I peek into the *bochurim*'s kitchen to see who is there. There is an old gray piano in the *bochurim*'s dining room where we all eat together sometimes. The back of the piano is open and I can see the strings move when I push the keys. Tatty knows how to play piano, and I like to hear him play.

I am too young, but I long to play piano too. I want to make music, to be creative. There is a restlessness inside of me.

I am four. The *bais medrish* is where the *Aron Kodesh* (Holy Ark) is, and where Zaidy, the uncles and the *bochurim* learn Torah all the time unless they are *davening* (praying). Girls are not allowed to go into the *bais medrish*. Ever.

I know I'm a big girl, four years old, and I am not supposed to talk to the *bochurim*.

Bochurim don't look at girls or talk to girls, except for sometimes, when Tatty and Zaidy aren't with me.

I stand outside the door of the *bais medrish* to watch the *bochurim* dance on *Simchat Torah*.

I watch Tatty, Zaidy and my uncles moving in a circle of black and white, everyone squeezed together, touching. The black shoes stomp. One foot forward, then one foot back. Stomp, STOMP! Stomp, STOMP! Some of the men's eyes are squeezed shut tight, some are open wide. I sense that these men are connecting to something bigger than all of us, something I can't see.

Their song is shaking the floor. Vibrating inside me.

"Emes, emes, emes, emes, emes, emes, emes, emes atah hu rishoin! Emes, emes, emes, emes, emes, emes, emes, emes, emes ata hu acharoin!"

"Truth, truth, truth, truth, truth, truth, truth, truth! Truth is the first thing! Truth, truth, truth, truth, truth, truth, truth, truth! Truth is the last thing!"

I hope the men won't stomp a hole right through the floor and fall down to the cellar.

I join the ladies and girls in throwing candy at the men, and the boys run and catch them. Uncle Moishe catches some for me.

The carpet room doesn't have carpet. It *used* to have carpet, that's why it is called the carpet room. The carpet came off before I was born. The couches in the carpet room are covered with dark red plastic, smooth, hard and cold. I have to go through the family dining room and the carpet room to go upstairs.

The stairs squeak when I climb them. In the morning, when I wake up in *yeshiva*, I walk down carefully so they don't make so much noise, because people are sleeping.

Omi, Zaidy's mother, lives in *yeshiva* too. She has her own living room and bedroom upstairs. There is a glass fish tank in her bedroom, with colored stones on the bottom, but no fish in it.

I know that no one is allowed to bother Omi.

I stay far away from Omi's and Zaidy's rooms. I walk past the bathroom and through the door at the end of the hall, to the stairs going up to the family's third floor.

The door to the *yeshiva* side, where the *bochurim's* bedrooms are, is open again. Mommy said it is supposed to be locked.

There are two shiny black dumbbells on the floor just inside the door. I'm not sure what they are for, or why they are so heavy, my small arms cannot lift one even an inch. One of the *bochurim* is hiding them on the family side so Zaidy won't know they're his. I peek in, but I don't go in there. I am not allowed to go in to the *bochurim's* dorms by myself.

The bad girl, the one who Tatty hurts at night, is sometimes left in there with the bochurim.

They give Tatty money, and she has to do what they say.

It hurts her backside, and she pushes her head hard into the wall so she won't feel anything.

She hears a child's voice crying in the distance. She tells herself that the child is not her, that nothing real is happening.

She knows that she is bad.

When they finally let her leave she walks out and suddenly I am back inside myself and know I shouldn't be on the bochurim's side of yeshiva. I feel confused.

By the time I leave, I have already lost the memory of what happened.

There are more stairs on the *bochurim's* side, going up to the *bochurim's* third floor which is separate from the family third floor. We sleep there sometimes on *Shabbos*, and also during the week when the *tantas* and uncles are watching us and there are no extra beds on the family side.

One time, Zaidy takes me and Hadassa upstairs, to the bathroom with the big bathtub that has animal feet. He leaves the door open and we can hear and see him use the toilet.

Zaidy likes it when we watch.

I glance at Hadassa and then quickly look away. She looks away too.

We are ashamed and scared. We know we are not supposed to watch people going to the bathroom. We never talk about it. Tatty is in charge of me, Gittel and Hadassa, because Mommy is taking care of our babies.

Tatty rents a motel room in the Holiday Inn so he can take us swimming in the indoor pool while Mommy rests. Sometimes Tatty's friend is there with his children. He used to learn in Zaidy's *yeshiva*. One girl has red hair and I like to play with her.

Things happen in the Holiday Inn that hurt and scare the bad girl inside me, the one who Tatty hurts at night. One time she jumps into the pool on purpose and falls under the water. She wanted to stop breathing so no one could hurt her anymore. Tatty pulls her out of the water before she drowns.

Tatty saves my life.

I am vaguely aware that there is a bad girl inside me, but I am sure she is not real. What happens to her is just like a bad dream. Like the dream I had when I was four and a black-clothed man on a black horse jumped through my bedroom window to hurt me. I tried desperately to move and I couldn't even blink. I woke up shaking and afraid to go back to sleep. On *Shabbos*, the dining room light is on all night and I never have bad dreams on *Shabbos*. It is the one night I can fall asleep without fear.

We don't get Chanukah presents because it's *goyish* (non-Jewish). Instead, we get new *Pesach* (Passover) toys every year. It is the best thing that happens in our house, besides *mishloach manos* (gifts of food) we get on the holiday of Purim. On Purim I get my own *mishloach manos* with all my favorite junk foods. One year I got a whole box of my favorite sugar cereal and a whole box of gum.

We always put the old toys away for Passover. We scrub them in the bathtub with soap and water. Even one tiny dot of *chametz* (leavened food) is not allowed on *Pesach*.

It's *erev Pesach* (eve of Passover) and I sit on my bed trying very hard to wait patiently. Tatty and Mommy are sorting through bags of toys, and when they are done they will bring my pile to me. I am happy and excited. I am so lucky to have parents who buy me new toys every year! But I am also scared and I don't know why. Tonight we will go to the yeshiva for the *Seder* (Passover ritual meal) like we always do. I love the *Seder* in yeshiva with my aunts and uncles. I sing the *Mah Nishtana* (Four Questions) by myself, and everyone claps. I get chocolate and I get to stay up late. *Erev Pesach* I am supposed to be taking a nap but I can't settle down. I have no memory of anything bad happening,

I just feel a sense of dread.

I'm four years old, and today it's just me and Tatty.

Tatty wants to show me the matzah on the third floor on the yeshiva side. The children are not allowed up here alone because we might touch the matzah, and it could break.

The matzah is spread out on brown paper on the bed and Tatty holds up a matzah to the light. "Isn't it beautiful?" he says. "The matzah this year is pure gold."

He puts me up on the bed next to the matzah and starts to take off my clothes.

Suddenly, I know he wants to hurt me.

My stomach hurts.

I suddenly know that this happened before, and I suddenly remember how much it's going to hurt.

I push my head into the wall and my eyes stare and stare at the black inside my head. My mind feels fuzzy and far away. From far away in my head, I know that Tatty is angry with me because I'm too small.

He has to cut me.

It's sharp.

It's my fault.

Is the matzah cutting me?

I think I'm bleeding.

What is happening to me?

Is Tatty real? Am I real?

Did I hurt myself?

Something hurts bad. Tatty is talking,

Get dressed and come downstairs. He walks out.

No Tatty, no! Don't go away! I need you!

I can't move.

But I have to move or I'll get in trouble.

I need Mommy, but I can't let her see what happened. No one can know how bad I am.

I am moving even though it hurts.

I am walking down the hall to the stairs.

I am still staring and staring. My eyes don't want to move.

Uncle Moishe comes up and sees me walking down the hall.

He is upset that I am up here by myself with the matzah.

He tells me to go downstairs right now.

Don't I understand what I was told? Why am I not listening?

I don't know.

I guess I didn't listen.

I guess I hurt myself.

I guess I did something very bad on erev Pesach.

I wish I could be dead and never have a body. I want to squeeze my neck so hard I'll be dead. I want to smash my head so hard I'll be dead. I wish I was never alive. I wish someone would kill me already. But I am scared to die because Hashem will hurt me worse. It's so scary to be hurt and bad. My throat hurts from being sad.

We are moving today! Tatty is going to teach second grade, and we are moving to a new house, in a new city. I run outside to see the big moving truck. There is a blue boy's bike leaning against the gray stoop in front of our house. I know it's a boy's bike because it has a bar. I climb up on the stoop and put my leg over the bar and sit on the seat. I am so big! Suddenly, the bike is falling. I fall off the seat and the bar hits hard between my legs. It hurts so much I can't breathe.

I jump up fast. I'll get in trouble for touching something that isn't mine.

I run inside so no one will know how the bike fell. I don't tell anyone that it hurts.

I never tell. It's my fault that I got hurt like that, anyway.

Our new apartment, in the city, is small, much smaller than our old house near *yeshiva*. We only have two bedrooms, one for the parents, and one for all the children: Gittel, Hadassa, me, Chaya, Tzvi and Devorah. Tanta Leah lives with us too. She sleeps at the front of the house in a room that used to be a porch.

An old lady named Mrs. Herman lives next door. The skin on her arms looks like it's falling off because she is so old. It wiggles when she moves. I felt it when she wasn't looking. It is so soft... I wish I could keep touching it. We are living in Mrs. Herman's house. She lets us live there because we pay her money. I learn that this is called renting.

In the morning Tanta Leah, Gittel and Hadassa all go to Bais Yaakov together on the city bus. I want to go too.

"Isn't there a place for kids my age to go?" I ask Mommy.

Mommy tells me that when I'm five, maybe I can go to kindergarten. In the meantime, she wants me home.

I look out the window of our new house and see something I never saw before. A little girl with *black skin* in the yard across the street from our new house. Her hands look dirty where I guess she tried to wash the black off. I feel so bad for her. I wonder what happened to make her dirty. Mommy tells me the girl was born that way. I wonder if the little black girl feels bad and dirty on the outside, like I do on the inside.

I am finally going to kindergarten at Bais Yaakov, three days a week! I'm so excited. I am going to have friends! I am going to have my own locker! I will have teachers and a playground with swings, and a new lunch box! I will finally go on the city bus in the morning with Tanta Leah and my big sisters. Mommy tapes a quarter into my lunch box to pay for the bus on the way home, when Tanta Leah won't be with me. Tanta Leah is in high school and comes home much later than kindergarten. I notice that the other girls in kindergarten look more real than I do. The other girls don't seem afraid. The other girls are cute. I am not cute. I wish I was cute like the other little girls. I like going to kindergarten even though I'm different from the other kids.

I wish I were real.

Tanta Leah is sick and some people bring her home from school early today. I go outside with Mommy and watch them bring her in. Two ladies are holding her arms and dragging her from the car into the house. Tanta Leah is crying and trying to run away.

One of the ladies who dragged her in closes all of the open cabinets in the kitchen, bang, bang, bang! I think she is angry because our house is messy.

Last night, Tanta Leah's friends from high school stayed over and gave her coffee to drink all night long. I hear Mommy say that Tanta Leah took too much of her medicine and it would be dangerous for her to fall asleep. If she doesn't want to go to the hospital, she has to stay awake.

Something scary happens in kindergarten. I am in the bathroom washing my hands, and the boy from the nursery class tells me to push open the door to one of the bathrooms. The boy's mother is a teacher, so that's why he learns in Bais Yaakov even though he's a boy.

I push open the door, and there is a girl sitting on the toilet. I didn't know that boy wanted me to do something bad! I didn't even know someone was in there.

The other children laugh. The girl yells that she is going to tell the teacher on me.

I am scared to go back to kindergarten, so I stay in the bathroom. The teacher has to come find me. I'm scared. I hope she won't tell Mommy. I don't want Mommy to know that I did something bad in a bathroom... again.

I never get angry. And I don't hit or bite. And I always listen. My sister, Hadassa, is very angry. She hits and bites a lot and she doesn't listen. Sometimes Mommy locks her in the basement. I hope that never happens to me. Today, Hadassa didn't listen to Mommy and wouldn't get in the bath. Tatty is angry with her. He's trying to take a nap.

Tatty told Hadassa that if he has to get up, he will throw her into the bath with all of her clothes on. Hadassa still didn't listen, and Tatty got up and threw her in the bath, kicking and screaming, with all of her clothes on. Then, he undressed her in the bath, and threw her down on her bed with nothing on. I hope Tatty won't hurt her. I never get angry and I never make Tatty angry.

I always listen.

Zaidy's study

We are moving back to *yeshiva* once again, because Zaidy wants us to. Zaidy never wanted us to leave *yeshiva* in the first place, so now we have to go back. According to Tatty, Zaidy is in charge and what he wants is what we do. I should be going into first grade, but there is no Jewish day school near *yeshiva* so we will learn at home with Mommy. Zaidy found us a new house near *yeshiva* with an underground pool in the backyard. Tatty is happy. He likes the pool. I love our new house too.

It is so big and so beautiful! It is on a dirt road in the woods, and cars hardly ever drive by. Sometimes only one or two a day. The kitchen has real carpet. I never saw a kitchen with carpet before and it seems very fancy. There is a peach tree in our yard, and horses down the block. Tatty named the horses *Fertel* and *Ferd*. (Little horse, and horse in Yiddish.) I can hear them snorting at night. Kittens, dogs and chickens live near us too.

Tatty buys us bikes and I learned to ride without training wheels. I can even ride with no hands. We ride around and around the poles in the big cellar when it is raining or snowing and we can't play outside. Tatty's learning room has a brick fireplace. The ceiling has what looks like long peanut chews stretched across it. The living room has a mirror covering an entire wall.

There are four bedrooms upstairs and each one has a different color soft carpet. I sleep in the room with the blue carpet with Hadassa. Gittel, Chaya and Devorah sleep in the bigger room with the orange carpet. Mommy and Tatty sleep in the room with the green carpet. The boys, Tzvi and my baby brother Shalom, sleep in the room with the yellow carpet.

It takes five minutes to walk from our new house to *yeshiva*, through the woods and across a soybean field. I run across the field breathing in the fresh air. I pick and taste the soybeans. They feel fuzzy on my tongue. I love being outside with the sky and the air and the trees and the soybeans. The *tantas* and the uncles come over every day. We play outside a lot. Tanta Yocheved plays kickball with us in the front yard. Mommy teaches us how to play "Kitty wants a Corner." She used to play it when she was a little girl. I'm good at it. We have a lot of time to play because we don't go to school. We made up some new games.

One new game is called "Monster." The "monster" gets the hallway and the kitchen. The "people" get the living room, dining room and Tatty's learning room. The people have to run across the kitchen and hallway without the monster tagging them. If the monster tags you in the kitchen or the hallway, then *you* have to be the monster and you have to try to tag someone else.

It's a scary and fun game.

We make up another game that we only play in the morning when Mommy is still sleeping, and we are hungry. The game is called "Party." Gittel and Hadassa take turns making things to eat. They mix funny things like yogurt with American cheese and blackstrap molasses. Then, me and Chaya and Tzvi have to taste it, or else we are out of the game.

We don't have other children to play with besides one cousin who is five, because we don't go to school and there are no neighbor children. If someone asks us at the grocery store why we aren't in school, we have to tell them we go to school in *yeshiva*. Otherwise Mommy and Tatty can get into trouble. It's against the law for children not to go to school.

Tanta Dassie brings Tanta Leah over holding her tight by her arm. She is acting sick again. She is sitting in the middle of the living room rug and crying. She is talking like a baby. It is up to the family to take care of her because *Chas v'shalom!* (heaven forbid!), if she is taken to the hospital and given drugs she will be turned into a zombie. That's why no one is allowed to know.

Mommy and her sisters all married Zaidy's *bochurim*, his boys. Zaidy is letting Tanta Leah marry one of his *bochurim* even though she is sick, and even though everyone says not to marry Avi because he is not good. Avi comes to our house dressed like a lady on Purim. He even smells like perfume. I thought he really was a lady until Mommy told me it was really Avi. Eww! But Tanta Leah will marry Avi anyway because she doesn't have a choice. Mommy says she has a condition. A chemical imbalance in her brain. And who else would marry her with her condition?

I am seven. Hadassah is eight. We sometimes go to the *yeshiva* for *shacharis davening* (morning prayers) with Tatty early in the morning. Zaidy likes it when we come.

Once, after davening, he takes us into his office.

He puts his hands under my clothes into my underwear. His finger hurts me and I look at him, shocked. "Don't look at me," he says. "Look at the sefarim" (the religious books).

I look at the glass doors, behind them rows of religious books, some of them too heavy to lift. I make my mind leave Zaidy's office so I won't feel or know about his finger in my underwear. What would he have seen had he looked into my eyes? What would I have seen had I looked into his? But I was taught to listen, and so I looked at the books, not at Zaidy.

After he is done, he asks me and Hadassah, "Do I need to get married again?"

He tells us that he loves one of us more than the other. I feel sad and confused. I know it is Hadassah he loves more and I am not sure why I am less lovable. I just know that I am. Then, Zaidy takes us to the toy store and tells me to pick out a toy. Any toy.

Shalom

We have to find a new doctor. Our pediatrician, Dr. Sharp, might go to jail and Mommy is sad because she likes Dr. Sharp. The police found his wife's dead body buried under the picnic table in their backyard. Mommy shows me the newspaper clippings that Gittel is collecting of all of the stories about his court case. She tells me that Dr. Sharp is a good doctor. He never tells her she has to give us medicine, even when we are sick. I hate medicine! Mommy thinks Dr. Sharp probably killed his wife in self-defense. She thinks his wife was abusive and was bigger than him anyway. If he wasn't going to jail she would still use him as our pediatrician. Zaidy likes Dr. Sharp, too. Zaidy was asked to testify for Dr. Sharp as a character witness. He won't do it because he says that given the right circumstances, anyone can do anything. I think that means Zaidy thinks Dr. Sharp really did it. I wish he would testify so I don't have to get another doctor who will tell Mommy to give me medicine.

My little brother Shalom calls me "Mommy." Mommy says it's because I love him so much and take such good care of him. He is so cute, and I pretend that I'm really his mother. Mommy told me she is going to have another baby soon.

"Don't stop giving Shalom attention when the new baby comes," Mommy told me. "He will be sad if you only pay attention to the new baby. He thinks you're his mother." I am six years old.

I promise Mommy and myself that I'll remember to give Shalom attention, even if the new baby is really cute.

Today I'm in yeshiva with Shalom and some other children.

I don't have any clothes on. None of the children do.

Tatty left us with the bochurim again.

I know the bochurim will hurt my body and I want to die before it happens.

But this time is different.

This time it's worse.

This time they want me to hurt Shalom first. I have to listen or they will hurt me even worse. But I can't listen. He is my baby and it's my job to take care of him. He thinks I'm his mommy.

My body is not safe because I'm a girl.

Boys are stronger than girls.

Boys are allowed to hurt people.

I need to be a boy RIGHT NOW.

RIGHT.

NOW.

I am a boy now. A very bad boy.

A boy can hurt children and likes to hurt children.

The bochurim put the boy's hand on Shalom's bris (circumcision) and I watch the boy squeeze him and twist him hard. Shalom screams. It's my fault. I should kill this bad boy. They put the bad boy on top of Shalom and I am bumping into him, hard just like they bang on me. Just like Tatty bangs on me.

I know Shalom can't breathe right and it hurts him. He is screaming.

The bad boy inside me doesn't care. He likes to hurt people. He is strong.

I didn't do it.

I would never hurt my baby. But I know it's really my fault.

They are laughing at me and looking at another girl inside me. Not me. It feels exciting. She is a bad girl because she likes it and deserves it, anyway. They keep touching her down there. I wish they would stop making her bad and just finish already.

Just kill me already.

The bochur is banging into my body so hard and I think I might die.

I'm too scared.

I hate my body.

I hope he kills it.

Make it dead and gone forever.

It hurts so bad.

I'm being broken in half.

All the way up to my mouth.

I will never be whole again.

I'm a broken icky girl.

I'm not screaming because I can't breathe.

But I'm glad they are hurting me, and not my baby.

I deserve it. It is my fault.

I deserve to be dead and broken.

They give me my clothes and tell me to get dressed, and to dress Shalom and go downstairs.

I can't move right away. Everything hurts.

I get dressed as quick as I can so no one will see the bad part of me.

I dress my baby Shalom and carry him downstairs.

He is quiet now, and I know he is scared and sad, just like me.

I am so sorry baby! I should have helped you! I should have saved you! I was supposed to take care of you. I am a bad mommy.

I am far away in my head and nothing hurts anymore. I decide inside that really nothing happened. It's time to go play Fisher Price… Fisher Price is a game I can control. I can build houses for the little people using books laid out as the floors of different rooms, and blocks for furniture, and act out all kinds of stories. It is fun and not scary.

I hold Shalom on my lap and sit on the couch in the carpet room. We sit together staring at nothing for a long time. Forgetting.

Before bedtime I have to change my underwear. I wish I didn't have to change. I wish I didn't have a body but I have no idea why I'm so upset. I wish I didn't have to be a girl. I need Mommy to help me but she can't help me. I hate my body but I don't remember why.

I can't get Mommy's help because then she will know how bad I am. Why do I feel so awful?

I bite my hand to try not to cry, but I can't help it and I start to cry, and then to scream but without making a single sound. I squeeze myself into a corner of the bathroom near the bathtub. I am screaming without a sound in the bathroom. I wait in the bathroom after I stop crying so my face will look normal and no one can tell. My head hurts. My eyes hurt. I can't sleep. And I don't know why.

I have terrifying dreams that something too big and heavy is squishing me flat until I can't breathe anymore. Then, in the dream, I die. I also dream that a monster suddenly hurts me and is going to kill me. I have the dreams again and again, and I try to stay awake all night so I won't have the horrible dreams. I always fall asleep in the end.

Shalom is always sick now, and Mommy is worried about him.

He can't breathe so well. I think it's because I squished him but I don't remember when I did that. His nose is always stuffed and he has to breathe through his mouth. He cries a lot now and is sad all the time. He used to be a happy baby. He used to be my baby. I don't like him so much now. I have an idea that it's because I'm bad, and I was supposed to watch him and I didn't. I think maybe a boy hurt Shalom once.

I think Tatty knows I am bad too. We share a secret, and we both need to pretend to Mommy that we don't know how bad I am.

Tatty loves me. He doesn't really want me to be hurt, and he doesn't want me to be bad. He can't help it that a part of me is bad. He doesn't want Mommy to find out about the bad part of me. Neither do I. But I think maybe Mommy knows, anyway, because she tries to keep me away from Tatty.

She told me I'm too big to sit on Tatty's lap at the *Shabbos* table. I am turning seven, and seven is too big. My head blocks Tatty's mouth.

I know she doesn't want Tatty to touch me anymore, because now I'm a big girl. Now I'm seven. Boys and girls are not allowed to touch.

PART 2:

FORGETTING

We are moving back to the city so that Tatty can teach again. I am eight years old. Tatty is an excellent teacher and the school wants him back. Savta wants us to move back to the city and go to school like other kids. Mommy tells me she wants to move too. I sense, or maybe she told me, that she doesn't want Zaidy to be in charge of Tatty anymore. She doesn't like the control that Zaidy seems to have over Tatty. I miss school, being with other children, but I don't want to move.

I love our big house with the pool and the trees, and flowers and horses. I tell Mommy that I will miss the trees too much, and she laughs, but not in a happy way. She tells me that I like trees and animals more than people. Apparently, I'm supposed to like people more.

I decide to change my name from Genendy to Genendel when I start school in third grade. It will be better if I am someone different. I will tell them my name is Genendel. That feels different.

I feel strange in my new school, Bais Yaakov, even though I was there a long time ago for kindergarten. The other children know each other and I don't. They also know more than I do about just about everything. They can write in Hebrew script and I can't. They know words like Inner Harbor and Holocaust, and I don't know what those words are. Sometimes they are mean to each other and I am afraid someone will be mean to me. I am always scared in school but no one knows. I can sense I am different from the other children.

I always wanted a boy doll, and I finally convince my mother to get one for *Pesach* when I am ten, but it is a shameful victory. I need a doll, this particular doll, and it has to be a boy.

The doll I want is named Mickey. I see 'him' (although he is not anatomically correct) in a toy magazine. I tell Mommy and my older sisters that

I want Mickey so I could learn to sew dolls' clothes. But I know that is not the real reason. The real reason is something I deny even to myself. I have a secret game that I play with Mickey. When no one is watching I take off his clothes. I yank his legs apart and bite him between his legs. I hate him and I want to hurt him. I don't know why I need to do that, I just do it. I hit him, and bang his head hard, and make him take his clothes off, even his underwear. Before I had Mickey, I used to do the same thing with my Curious George, because he was also a boy. But Mickey is better. More real.

I have no idea why I play in this way. I am just angry at boy dolls, and I know that if anyone saw my game they would know that something is wrong with me.

Tatty tells me that I am very lucky that I learned to read, because he thinks I have dyslexia, which is probably why it was so hard for me to learn to read English.

I learned to read Hebrew when I was five and it was much easier. Tatty says if Mommy and Tanta Leah hadn't worked so hard to teach me how to read I would probably have to be in a special class in Bais Yaakov for children who can't read. That would be really embarrassing. I learned to read and I can't stop. I never have enough books. I feel like I am also not so real, like the characters in the books, and that's why I like to read so much.

I become whoever I am reading about, and as long as my book lasts I exist. Mommy senses that I become real through books and it bothers her. She doesn't understand why they are so important to me. She doesn't like that I read so much.

I need books to escape my inner world. I need them to survive.

The Actress

I'm in the fourth grade, and I am trying on my friend's glasses. Suddenly I can see the blackboard more clearly.

I tell Mommy that I think I need glasses.

Mommy says, "No you don't. You see well enough."

In fifth grade I borrow a book, *Tomboy*, from my friend Shani. It is about a girl my age getting her period. Mommy catches me reading the book at night and takes it away. It isn't modest to read about girls' private bodies.

The next morning Tatty tells me he has to speak to me about something very serious. He tells me that reading books like *Tomboy* is like eating pig. It's *traif* (not kosher). It's a terrible thing to do.

Mommy won't give the book back and I'm embarrassed, scared and ashamed. From now on Tatty or Mommy will be checking all of my books before I read them, even the ones from the Bais Yaakov library. And I am not allowed in the public library without a parent along to chaperone. I know it is for my own good. I cannot be trusted.

I am lucky that Mommy and Tatty love and care about me so much.

Although I am only ten, I am told that I am very mature and responsible for my age. My mother's friend and neighbor hires to me babysit her three children when she teaches Sunday school - two girls and a boy, ages two, three, and eight. The eight-year-old is my assistant and we are close friends. We play creative, imaginary games together, and she admires and looks up to me. I feel good about taking care of the children, feeding them and making sure they are safe and happy. Even changing diapers doesn't bother me, something Mommy never asks me to do at home, and I'm making some money to spend, too.

My fifth grade teacher sends home a note telling my mother to get my eyes checked, because I can't see the board. I have to squint. Mommy tells me gently that she still does not want to get me glasses. She doesn't think I really need them. She thinks I'm exaggerating. But in the end, she gives in.

"I am getting you glasses in order to get the teacher off my back, not because you need them," she tells me. I overhear Tatty talking to the eye doctor after he checked my eyes. They send me out of the room so I wouldn't hear, but I hear anyway.

"…We really want her playing outside more… She's always reading…"

I hear the doctor's voice. He sounds surprised. "I can see by the shape of her pupils that Genendy is very nearsighted. Do you want your daughter walking around in a blurry world?!"

I can't hear what Tatty says back, but I guess they do. And I don't understand it.

How can it be that I see much better with glasses if I don't really need them? Could it be true that I just want them for attention?

My brothers and sisters laugh at me and make fun of my glasses.

"Mommy said you don't really need them. You just want to be like her," Hadassa teases.

Hadassa hates me. I feel ashamed and confused. But I remind myself that I am actually very lucky. I have everything I really need. I have God and the Torah, and parents who are alive and brothers and sisters to play with. I have a very happy life. I don't understand what's wrong with me. Mommy says I have no reason to ever be sad or angry. She thinks I make things up all the time. Just like I made up needing glasses.

She tells me, "Genendy, you make up stories. You're such an actress."

I ask her if she will believe me that I need glasses when I'm *bas mitzvah* (coming of age at 12 years), because then I can never lie because it would be a big sin. She laughs and says no. Being *bas mitzvah* won't help her believe me.

Mommy is very strict about bedtime. Everyone has to sleep in their own bed. The girls sleep upstairs and the boys sleep downstairs, down the hallway from Tatty and Mommy's room. No boys are allowed upstairs and sharing a bed is never allowed. Sometimes we sneak into each other's beds before we fall asleep to talk and play. I tell my younger sister Chaya awful stories.

The girls in my stories are forced to take their clothes off, and they are laughed at. They are forced to eat their own vomit. Their private parts are cut off and hung up so everyone could see how gross and disgusting they are. My stories are terrible and I know they aren't true and I shouldn't be telling them. But I need to tell them to someone. Because I need to express my anger and shame. And the experience of violation that is inside me.

But I know that I am not making up *all* these stories. Terrible things actually happened to the bad parts of me.

Jay

My muscles are alive. The sound of blades scraping ice, and cool air blowing against my face, blowing my long denim Biz skirt between my legs. My lithe 12-year-old body rejoices in movement and balance. I look down and it looks like I'm wearing jeans, which I am never allowed to wear. I speed around the rink, faster, faster, and slow down as I turn the corner. Multi-colored disco lights dance to Miami Boys Choir that our *B'nos* (girls' group) leader asked the rink to substitute for the usual pop music. We rented the place out and are entitled to our choice of music. I ignore the swish of long skirts, the giggles and shouts of middle and high school Bais Yaakov girls skating all around me. I breathe and feel my heart pumping, so alive. This is a rare experience. It's not just that I have never ice-skated before. What is really unusual for me is feeling okay in my body, and I cherish the moment.

There is a sudden flash on the ice in front of me, a piece of jewelry, a bracelet, that must have fallen off someone's wrist. My ankle twists as my skate blade contacts the bracelet, and I am sliding across the ice on my side, a searing pain radiating up my ankle to my knee. I can't move. Two twelfth grade girls slide up beside me.

"Need a hand?" they ask.

I nod but I don't reach up to grab their hands. I'm afraid, so afraid of the pain and the loss of control of my body and of being hurt. I am hesitant to let them touch me, to admit I am hurt and vulnerable. I don't want to be hurt but at the same time it feels so right.

"I think I broke my leg," I say, and it sounds right, too. Finally, my inner brokenness can be seen and felt. My inner pain is suddenly real in my injured ankle. The girls pull me up as I wince, unable to place my foot on the ice. I don't know where the shame comes from, the terror… and the relief. I'm hurt and that's good, but I am not supposed to be hurt. Being hurt is not and never was real.

Years later, when I am 18, I will remember this experience and will begin to make sense of these feelings. All I know now is that it should not be a relief for my 12-year-old self to be hurt, and yet I am relieved. What is the matter with me? Did I make this happen? My young brain rages in pain and confusion. I don't know or understand anything about triggers and flashbacks. I just know that, once again, there is something wrong in my reaction. I know somewhere deep inside that being hurt is my fault, my own doing, my responsibility. I should offer my mother to pay for the surgery I need to put my cracked bone back in place. Not that I have the money, but I know I am responsible and I need to pay. So I offer her 20 dollars to pay for the crutches.

I get lots of attention, treats and visitors, and that just makes me feel even more guilty. A sweet older male teacher from school brings me chocolate-covered orange peel, and we all have a good laugh over it. Who would eat orange peel?! Tanta Rivka drives in and brings me a personalized piggy bank full of candy, and helium balloons. My mother gives me vitamins, calcium and dolomite, and makes sure I eat healthy food.

My leg has healed, but I can tell that something is still very broken and scary inside of me. Outside too. Scary changes are happening to my body. Mommy says I'm growing up. Everyone can tell that I'm a girl and it's disgusting and frightening.

I try tying belts around my chest so no one can tell. I wear a really small tight bathing suit under my clothes. It flattens my chest and I feel safer that way. I wish I could find a way I could get an operation to change myself to a boy. Then maybe I would feel safe. I decide I really am a boy, then I feel safer. The boy part of me loves running, playing baseball, climbing, building, and breaking things. He built a treehouse. I sometimes think Tatty must realize that part of me is a boy because he bought him a Robotics set. Tatty also plays catch with him in the back yard.

Sometimes nothing feels real, and I don't believe my parents are my real parents. I don't think Tatty and Mommy know about these other parts of me. I think they only see the girl they call Genendy. It's weird but sometimes the boy inside me feels more real than I do. We hate being trapped in a girl's body.

I call my boy part Mr. Nobody because I know he's not real. He is Nobody.

He has his own thoughts and feelings. He thinks it's disgusting and embarrassing to always have to hide and pretend to be Genendy. He wishes my parents could know about him so that they could help him/me/us figure out why he is in my body, and who Genendy really is. I'm so angry inside and I hate myself. Sometimes I hurt myself on purpose. I have to find a way to get rid of my body or turn it into a boy's body. Boys are stronger and safer, and also, they are allowed to hurt people. I feel like God is punishing me to have made me be a girl, in Genendy's gross body.

I hate her, yet, somehow, I am her.

Sometimes I wonder if I'm adopted, or if I had a twin who died, because I feel like an important part of me is missing. Something sad and scary must have happened to me. But when I think back, nothing bad or scary ever really happened that I can remember. There is something, though. A dark place in my head that I never go into, except when I'm falling asleep. When I'm falling asleep I can't help it and I fall right in there. There are hurt children in this dark place in my mind, and they cry a lot. They are bleeding and naked. I cry with them, but I don't understand why they are there. I know they are not real. I am scared and confused. The hurt children and their feelings feel so real, and so sad. The boy part of me feels so real.

Even though I ignore these parts of me during the day, I am too distracted in school to concentrate. I need an adult to help me with these children, someone no one can hurt and is not scared of anything. I need a strong man. Someone who is not Jewish, because these hurt children in my head are not Jewish. The things that happened to them are *goyish*. They could never happen to a Jewish child.

So I make up a man to help me and call him Jay. He is big and strong. He is very angry and will kill anyone who tries to hurt these children again. He is not scared of anything. He takes the hurt children into a special house in my mind that is safe. He is a doctor and can fix them… But sometimes he has to hurt them and touch them too in order to help them.

I am writing a book about Jay to make sure I remember that he is there. I need him to stay with me. I am learning how to write from reading other books, and sometimes copying parts that speak to me. I especially love the *Black Stallion* series. In one book in the series a boy and his horse are in a plane accident and they both survive but the boy suffers from amnesia. I copy that part down, feeling like the boy is me, but knowing that of course he isn't. Something about the idea of amnesia resonates as real for me. It's so hard to get the books I need, because of my parents' rules. I want to scream at my mother, don't keep taking the books away from me! I need books!

There is a little boy who sometimes comes into my, Genendy's, room, and screams into her pillow.

He got hurt somewhere in the dark place. I never talk to my parents about this. But having Jay helps me. I can finally go to sleep every night without feeling like I am going to die.

Jay is going to stay with me for a long time. When I grow up and go to therapy, I will be shocked to learn that Jay is still with me. Even though I will realize that I made him up, he didn't know! (Neither did any of the other characters in my brain, for that matter.)

I think I am crazy, but meanwhile he takes on a life of his own. Many years from now, I will learn that Jay was my hero. My therapist will show me that Jay saved my life.

I am at my Bais Yaakov Junior High School's annual Purim party dressed in a costume that hides everything but my eyes. An older woman in a red tinseled wig, someone's grandmother I guess, sits down beside me to watch the show.

"Whose mother are you?" She smiles at me through my mask.

"Why do you assume that I'm a mother?" My voice is muffled.

She smiles kindly. "Your eyes give you away, dear. They're old."

My eyes are old.

I am only 12.

I have been sick for about a month. At night, I wheeze and gasp for breath. My mother thinks it's nothing serious. She hates taking us to the doctor. She doesn't trust doctors. They don't know everything; after all, they accidentally killed her mother. I'm worried that I am dying of some strange disease.

My mother finally decides to take me to the campus doctor at the local *yeshiva*. We happen to be going there anyway, and Mommy said maybe this is one of the few times I really do need antibiotics. The doctor says I have pneumonia. He can hear the rattling and wheezing so clearly in both of my lungs he doesn't need to bother sending me for a chest x-ray.

That is a huge relief - not having pneumonia but avoiding a chest x-ray. The thought of taking my shirt off and having anyone see my body is unbearable. The doctor writes a prescription for antibiotics. I am relieved that Mommy actually fills it.

My baby brother, Yehudah, catches pneumonia as well and is given antibiotics within a day.

Until I get married, I have to listen to my parents. After I marry, I will have to listen to my husband. Girls in our community don't learn Talmud, so they don't know things like boys and men do. We have to ask.

My aunts and uncles all married and moved to a nearby town. We visit them often. On one visit, I see Uncle Moishe slap his eight-year-old son in the face. I always thought Uncle Moishe was a kind and gentle man. My cousin looks stunned. He doesn't even blink or cry.

"How can you hit your child in the face like that?!" I ask Uncle Moishe.

He shrugs. "My father used to hit *me* in the face, and I'm fine," he says calmly.

You are not fine if you can slap your child in the face, I think to myself but do not say out loud.

Juggling

One thing that helps me feel a sense of control over my body is doing gymnastics. I learned how to stand on my head as a third grader. I begged my mother to send me to a gymnastics class so I could gain skills and get really good at it, but she won't allow it. The local JCC has all girls' gymnastics and trampoline classes, but men and boys walk in and out, and if one of them stuck his head in, it just wouldn't be modest. So I teach myself what I can. I can turn cartwheels, walk on my hands, and do flips. I practice almost every day. I feel strong and powerful in my body when I practice. But I can't get past a certain point without any guidance, so I look for other ways to feel a sense of control in my body.

I always admired Uncle Moishe's ability to juggle three balls. I am bored and my mother doesn't like me leaving the house. She doesn't like my friends. She doesn't like me participating in after-school activities. She doesn't let me go to the library. I confront her with my boredom. She suggests I teach myself to juggle, so I do. My parents give me a juggling book for *Pesach*. I can't get enough of juggling. It's like a metaphor for my life. And I have a book now that can teach me and help me master a lot of tricks. I have to concentrate and work hard and use my muscles. I am obsessed with juggling. I break a glass picture frame and a light but my mother doesn't get upset. She is just glad that I'm busy and home, where she can keep a close eye on me. I learn to juggle balls, rings, clubs, and five balls on my own. I can bounce juggle and juggle lying on my back and eating an apple. I teach Hadassa, Chaya and Tzvi to juggle, and Chaya and I can juggle seven balls, passing them back and forth between us. When I'm juggling my mind is free.

Colorful balls fly from the juggler's fingers…
Impossibly they are flowing through the air
Barely missing each other as they skim past
A dazzling enigma
I pick up the balls and toss them too in a colorful arc
One two three fall
One two three crash
I want to give up
Now just once more
One two three four
Suddenly, amazingly, there is order in the chaos
My heart leaps and jumps with the balls.
Then crash
My hands are empty but my heart is full
For a moment I saw the pattern.

Depression

I am 15, but inside I actually feel strangely all different ages. Tanta Leah and Uncle Avi move into our house, together with Zaidy. Tanta Leah is sick again and she is living with us so that we can take care of her five children. The house is stuffed. My six-year-old cousin is sharing my tiny room that only has room for one bed. Her mattress on the floor is halfway under my bed. She climbs into my bed at night because she is scared. I love that they live with us. I also hate it.

I love to be useful and to be helping, and distracted from my inner turmoil. Mommy says I have to help in any way I can. These children really need me because they have no one. Their father and mother can't take care of them right now. I have jobs, like patting my baby cousin's back until he goes to sleep. If I don't do it, he bangs his head against the crib until he falls asleep.

He has bruises on his head. I can't take care of the children inside me very well, but I can help these children. And unlike the children inside me, these children are real.

I know I'm not supposed to complain, but the truth is, I don't like that they took over our house and our lives. Nothing else is important to any of the adults. The drama is endless. I sometimes imagine I am in a T.V. show. My aunts and uncles hate Avi and kicked him out of the house because they say he makes Tanta Leah sick. Hadassa hates Avi and does things to annoy him on purpose, like stealing his towel. Avi will not use a towel that anyone else touched. He has a lot of rules like that.

Hadassa thinks she is fat and is always trying not to eat so much. Mommy is very worried about Hadassa's eating habits. Last week they were arguing about food and she said to Hadassa, "Just watch Genendy, she never worries about what she eats. Just eat what she does."

I wish Mommy hadn't said that. Now Hadassa stares at me when I eat. Now *I* can't stop thinking about what I eat. I decide I can only allow myself one protein, one carbohydrate, and fruits and vegetables every day. I feel better inside, even though I'm starving.

Zaidy is in the kitchen where Mommy and Tanta Leah are preparing *Shabbos* food for our families. The delicious smell of fresh challah, chicken, and kugel arrives in the kitchen every week like clockwork. "Ask your sister for forgiveness," Zaidy tells Aunt Leah.

"For what Daddy?"

"Because as a young child she would get hit because you cried."

Tanta Leah turns to Mommy.

"Will you forgive me?"

"Yes, of course."

Zaidy nods. "Good."

Mommy tells me that when she was a child Zaidy hit too much out of anger. He hit her until she was married. After she got married, Mommy was afraid to let Zaidy into the house because she worried he might still hit her. After Mommy's mother, Bubby, died, when Mommy was 15, the hitting got a lot worse. If the baby, Tanta Leah, who was three, cried and Mommy couldn't keep her quiet, she was hit by Zaidy. She had to try really hard to keep Tanta Leah quiet.

Uncle Baruch and Uncle Shmulie tried to protect Mommy and stop Zaidy from hitting her so much. The *tantas* and uncles were afraid of Zaidy, and of Omi too.

Omi moved into the *yeshiva* after Bubby died, and she was very strict. Mommy tells me she once peeked into a bag that was on the table, curious what was in there, and Omi sharply reprimanded her, calling her a nosybody.

I am 16, I am failing school. I am seriously depressed, and I know I need help. I decide to take a risk and tell my mother.

"I think I need to see a therapist."

"Why?" she asks. I had a feeling this wouldn't go well.

"Because I'm depressed."

"What do you mean by depressed?"

I can't answer her question. I don't have the words to explain to her that my inner and outer worlds are in chaos. Nor would I dream of telling her about the young children inside my mind, who are bleeding and hurt. I would never tell her that I had to make up a strong man, Jay, to take care of them. She'll think I'm crazy. I can't tell her that the dramas of my aunt struggling with bipolar, and my uncle and cousins living with us, are just too much for me. I am expected to help take care of the children every day. I am also expected to take care of my aunt when she has a manic episode. I know they need help and I want to do the right thing. I truly like them and I really do want to help.

So I say nothing. But I feel shame in asking for help and not being taken seriously. I tell myself I am stupid for hoping that my mother would believe me and get me the help I need.

My Bais Yaakov principal calls me out of class to tell me I'm failing high school. I already know that. He asks me what I am planning to do about it.

I tell him I'm not planning to do anything. My education is worthless to me, and I don't care. I hate the focus on my grades. Can't they tell something is wrong?

The principal tells me that I shouldn't think that just because my mother and her sisters got *shidduchim* (marriage prospects) without an education that I will as well. I am to realize that *their* father was a *rosh yeshiva* (head of the yeshiva). My father is not a *rosh yeshiva*, and had no *talmidim* (students) for me to marry.

I stare at him. A *shidduch*? Is he serious? I doubt I will survive long enough to worry about a *shidduch*. My breath is getting stuck on the way down. I'm afraid I'm going to cry.

For a moment, I imagine standing up and running out of the room.

I want to run as fast as I can past the playground, the basketball courts and the softball field into the forest and never come back. Ever. But in reality they would probably follow me and catch me. Or they wouldn't follow me and that would be even scarier. I am trapped and I burst into tears. I hate myself for crying. I have a rule that I am not allowed to cry in front of anyone. I am so embarrassed and ashamed. The principal calls the guidance counselor to stay with me. I ask her to leave the room. I would rather cry alone. I have to get away now. Away from home and school. As far away from my family and myself as I can get without falling off the planet.

My two-year-old baby cousin, Shaya, eats anything he can get his hands on. His little stomach is tight as a drum. Still, he eats more. We can't keep food out on the table because he will always eat it. He also runs away.

A stranger calls social services when she finds him in the middle of the street. She describes Tanta Leah as "drugged." This is an accurate description. She needs help. That's why she is living with us. I start hearing stories from Shaya, stories about Avi that make me want to cry - and throw up.

"Tatty made me go to the bathroom on the bed and then he rubbed it all over me and in my hair," Shaya tells me. "He squeezes me here." He touches his genitals. "I'm an icky, bad boy. I don't want to visit Tatty. He put a tree in my behind. It hurt me."

I feel sick to my stomach. His pain and shame are too familiar to me. I have flashes of hands touching me. Disgusting hands, like the ones touching him.

I'm having panic attacks.

My aunt and her lawyer give me a tiny tape recorder and ask me to get Shaya to tell his stories again so they can have it for court. I am the only one he talks to about this.

I am depressed that no one is protecting my cousins. I am tired of being invisible. I can't stay home another minute. We have children sleeping in every room, including the boiler room. One night, rust from the pipe in the boiler room falls into my little brother Yehudah's eye, and he has to have emergency surgery to have it removed. My father and I stay with him in the hospital overnight. The whole situation is crazy. I feel so trapped.

My life is a prison. My parents check everything I read, but do not do the same for my sisters. Gittel has a radio, but I am not allowed one. My mother took my stereo, without telling me what she was doing, and had the radio "professionally" broken. I suspect she caught me listening to *The Newlywed Game,* but I can only guess as there was no discussion. I came home from school to find my stereo gone. When I asked where my stereo went, my mother informed me that she was having the radio disconnected so I couldn't listen to it, and then she would give it back.

I beg my parents to let me go to Israel for the holiday of Sukkos. Tatty says if I pass all my next tests he will let me go. I know once I leave I won't come back.

Mommy hates the idea of going to school in Israel. She says that children who leave home at my age are usually missing something important later on. Something in maturity.

But I convince them to let me stay in Israel.

I don't think I can ever come back.

Bnei Brak

I am living with my great-aunt and uncle in Bnei Brak in Israel. They raised 16 children in a three-bedroom apartment. Many of the children are already married, but it is still cramped. I live out of a suitcase. I haven't seen a single toy in the house yet, but the children do not seem to feel lacking. They play with dirt, rocks, words, ideas.

I guess money isn't everything.

My great-uncle is a *dayan* (judge in the rabbinic courts). He and my great-aunt seem to have something otherworldly fueling their bodies. They are both tall and thin and bright eyed. They seem to float or dance, rather than walk around their apartment. It takes my uncle ten minutes to recite a blessing. He stutters on each word.

My great-aunt and uncle do not listen to music during the week. They also do not use any electricity or even flush toilets on *Shabbos*. My great-aunt koshers her own chickens in the sink near the tub. She is surprised that my mother doesn't kosher her own chickens. They take *frum* to a new level.

I try very hard to close myself off to the other girls in my class and ignore them. I sit in the classroom in a fog, grateful that I don't understand the language and don't have to speak to anyone. The truth is, I started to understand Hebrew, but I pretend I don't. It is a good strategy to keep people away.

Chedva, a girl in my class, is very persistent. She is the most popular kid in the class. She is always pushing herself through the fog into my world. What does she want with me? When I ask her, she tells me that she is bored. I give up trying to keep her away. It takes too much energy.

I accept an invitation to her house for *Shabbos*, and now I often spend *Shabbos* with her. She lives right behind the Vishnitz *yeshiva*. Friday night we go to the *tish* (rebbe's table). We push through a wall of women until we reach a hole in the lattice and peek down at a sea of men in black and white below us. The first time I watch through that lattice, I have to bite the inside of my cheek to check if I am really awake.

A long white table runs down the center of the room, with bleachers going up to the ceiling on either side. Married men and *bochurim*, with long swinging *peyos* (sidecurls), crowd on to the bleachers shoulder to shoulder, swaying and singing in unison. Around the table below sit bearded older men in round fur *shtreimels* (hats).

The rebbe sits at the head, in a throne-like chair, conducting the proceedings. He is wearing a shiny colored *bekisha* (long black coat). He is offered a tray of food, tastes a morsel, and passes a piece of food to the first man on his right. The men then pass the morsel hand over hand until it reaches the person it is intended for. By the time it gets to where it is going it often changes to a grayish color.

The recipient eats it anyway. It is *sherayim* (leftovers) from the rebbe. Holy food.

Holding his palm parallel to his nose, the rebbe slowly shakes his hand outward away from his face. His devoted Hassidim respond by waving back in the same manner.

The rebbe's assistant climbs up on the table in his white-stockinged feet. He is given a box of fruit and he tosses the fruit up at the bleachers where they are snatched from the air like fly balls at a baseball game. The lucky men who catch a fruit hold up their prize in victory. The peels are tossed back down over the heads of the men below, on to the table.

I'm pretty sure I'm awake.

We go to sleep to the sound of the singing which lasts all night long.

The singing is beautiful.

We bake *matzah* (unleavened bread) on the roof at midnight - my great-aunt and uncle, together with their children, sons-in-law and daughters-in-law, and me. The men and boys picked and ground the wheat themselves. My great-uncle oversees the entire operation. The teenage boys make the dough, just flour and water. The women roll it out, and the men push and pull the wooden poles with the *matzah* from the hot oven. They built the oven themselves.

My uncle holds a stopwatch aloft carefully counting down the minutes.

"*Kinderlach, kinderlach, shnell!*" he shouts, clapping his hands and his stopwatch together.

After each cycle of under 18 minutes the women wash and change the tables, their aprons, and everything else that came in contact with the dough. The poles are sanded down and the next cycle begins.

I have never seen anything like this.

Zaidy is coming to Israel for a very short visit. He will stay less than 24 hours and he wants me to spend time with him.

He is taking me to see his friend and mentor Rav Shlomo Zalman Auerbach. I sit out in the hallway while Zaidy speaks with the rabbi. They speak in Yiddish. The door is open and I can see and hear, if not understand, everything that is said.

.

Zaidy is very upset about my aunt Leah, who is going through a painful divorce from Avi. Zaidy breaks down and cries like a baby with Rav Shlomo Zalman.

"Mein tochter... Mein tochter..." My daughter, my daughter.

I expect Rav Shlomo Zalman to reach out and try to comfort Zaidy who is obviously in a lot of pain. Instead, Rav Shlomo Zalman says something to him in a sharp, angry voice. Rav Shlomo Zalman is clearly unhappy with something Zaidy has done, or is doing. I try not to eavesdrop. After a few minutes Zaidy calms down and the two speak quietly.

Then Zaidy calls me in, and asks Rav Shlomo Zalman to give me a blessing. The blessing I receive is that things will be good for me in the future. I will marry a good man. I will have good children. Life will be good.

I don't think that this sage, Rabbi Shlomo Zalman, has any idea what my life is like when he gives me this blessing. I don't know if I will survive one more day, let alone get married and have children.

Many years from now, though, I will recall this encounter and be comforted that he yelled at Zaidy, treating him like the real person, the flawed person, that he was.

Chedva

Chedva's pale face stays with me after I left Israel right before the Gulf War. When she learned I had to go home, even though I didn't want to, she said crying, "You will never come back. Once you get home your parents will never let you leave. I'm sure of it." I promised her I most certainly would come back. My parents had assured me I could come back once the danger was over.

Once I am home, I am told I am not going back so fast.

I am shocked, but I shouldn't have been.

For weeks I try to talk with my parents about Chedva, left alone in Bnei Brak. I tell them about her mother, and how abusively she treats her. Chedva and her siblings call her mother "The Gestapo." Chedva's mother hates her. She hits her regularly. She often tells me that Chedva was a very bad girl before I showed up. She had started showing interest in boys. Her mother is very grateful for what she saw as my positive influence.

I am good, Chedva is bad.

The more my parents hear about Chedva, her mother, and our close-friendship, the less they want me to have anything to do with her. They tell me they have no intention of letting me go back to Israel.

I write Chedva every day and she writes me back from Israel. Her letters become more and more depressing. She talks openly of ending her life. I show the letter to my father.

"If I were there, I could help her," Tatty says. "But I'm not there."

I beg, "I have to go back, Tatty. I promised her I would come back...And I need her just as much as she needs me."

Tatty's answer is firm. "We don't think it's a good situation for you. We are your parents and we know what's best for you. You have to trust us. We know what we're doing."

I try to get through to my mother.

"You don't understand!" I plead. "She is my best and only friend, and she needs me! You tricked me into coming home! You never intended to let me go back."

Mommy's silence is all the validation I need. She finally asks, "If I had told you that you could not go back would you have come home?"

"No."

That is the truth. I lock myself in the basement bathroom and cry. And I stop arguing because it isn't getting me anywhere.

I spend weeks in bed, too depressed to move or think. My arms and legs are weighted with lead. So is my mind. My parents buy me a book on self-esteem. It gives me some ideas. I realize that I am deeply depressed and it is hard for me to move. I try telling myself positive things as suggested in the book. "I am a good, kind, caring, worthwhile person." It is my new mantra. I don't believe it, but I can say it, and saying it ten times helps me get up and walk to the bathroom and back to bed. Another ten times saying "I am a good, kind, caring, worthwhile person" helps me walk downstairs. Repeating my mantra over and over, I manage to find an envelope and stamp and walk five minutes to the mailbox to mail a letter I wrote yesterday to Chedva. Then I slowly walk home and crawl back into bed exhausted.

A new job

One morning, my mother wades through the mess in my room and the fog in my head to inform me that she signed me up for a teacher job in the same school where my father worked, an all-boys religious elementary school, and I start tomorrow.

It is not a choice, she says. They need me and are expecting me. I am to work at the school's on-site babysitting service, caring for a group of two- and three-year-old children of the school staff. I go although I can barely move.

I go to work early with my father, my brothers Tzvi and Shalom, students in the school, and my two older sisters, Gittel and Hadassah, who teach in the pre-school. We arrive half an hour before the children do. At 8AM, as the first one there, I lie down on the industrial rug in the still dark room exhausted from the strain of getting up, dressed, and out of the house.

But the children will soon arrive and it is my job to keep them safe and happy, so I force myself to stand up and smile. I am not expected to do planned activities with them, which is a blessing, as standing up and smiling takes more than enough effort. I work with two other women who are in charge of the infants. They are in an adjoining room separated by glass windows. The door between the two rooms is closed during nap time so that my rambunctious toddlers, whose parents forbade me to let them sleep, would not disturb the napping babies.

I show up every day, which is the hard part. Yet, part of me likes being at work, in this room, where there is no past and no future, just bright colors, toys, and lively two- and three-year-olds. I spend a lot of time observing as I don't have energy to do much else. I am aware that parts of myself are floating somewhere in outer space, connected to my job and the children by the force of my parents' will that I function despite the debilitating depression.

One morning I wake up groggy and grope for my glasses on my desk. My mother doesn't like the fact that I need glasses and caring for my eyes has been an ongoing struggle. I went through a period of only having one lens in ninth grade. The other one fell out and Mommy was reluctant to fix it. I developed a convergence insufficiency as a result of trying to see through one eye. I recently got a new prescription and a new pair of rimless frames. I am very nearsighted and these new glasses are a hard-won celebration. I can finally see clearly. But my glasses aren't there this morning. They must have fallen. I reach down under the bed, peering close at the floor, then the desk. Nothing. I grope around for a few more minutes and then fish out my old, too weak pair, and put them on. Downstairs I tell my mother, "I can't find my new glasses."

"I know," she says calmly. "I took them." I gaze at her silently. Letting it sink in. Why would she do that?

"Why?" I ask, finally.

"They look too thick," she explains.

"Ma, they're rimless, so they look thicker. They help me see clearly. My vision is blurry in my old ones." I don't believe this.

"No. I'm keeping them. I want you to wear your old ones. I think the new ones are too strong."

The next day I visit a glasses store in the mall. I have my eyes examined and my proper prescription filled in a new pair of round black frames which I pay for myself. No more rimless ones for me.

I wear the new glasses home. Neither of my parents says a word but they both look rather shocked. Something is shifting, we all realize. I am as determined as always to try to take care of myself in spite of my parents' limitations. Only now I am no longer hiding.

Children

I have been working with children for several months, and I am beginning to find it energizing. Our room is the only world for these toddlers, here and now with me. They need me to be in the present with their tiny tables and chairs, their peanut butter crises and squabbles, and not lost somewhere in my head. They pull me into their present, rich, sensory world of play dough, friends who hug and then bite, and comfort objects, and away from my personal demons and toward connection and life. The parents like and trust me, and one even offers me an after-hours babysitting job. Does anyone notice how depressed and troubled I am?

One day this poem about the children comes pouring out of me.

What's in a child of two or three?
With everything left to do and see?
Touch and smell, taste and lick,
Hop and twirl, skip, jump, kick!
Climb and crawl, run and throw
So many things he has to know
Wiggle and squirm, giggle and shout
Discover what his world is all about
Pretender, inventor of novel ideas
Full of curious questions and unabashed fears
Tender and loving, never judging
Knows what he means, knows what he wants
Knows how to tantrum, piercing shrieks and stomps!
Yet simple moments bring him intense delight
He lives each present feeling with all of his might
Look at a child, wonder and guess
How he cries and laughs in the same short breath.
With boundless energy, he plays through the day

Perceiving reality in his own unique way.
What's in a child of two or three?
What is it I sense that he can teach me?

The words come faster than I can write them down. Reading what I had written, I realize that I am in love with these children, and with teaching. I am learning from the children how to live. These beautiful pure souls, these innocent children with their tiny bodies and huge minds of unimaginable potential, are my teachers. With them I not only discover my teacher-soul, my calling, but I also forging a path to sanity and life.

Running away

I am running away from home.

This is the scariest thing I have ever done. All I have with me is a small maroon handbag. Inside is one change of clothes, some snacks, cash, and a little book of phone numbers. That's it. My parents think I am babysitting tonight and they are not very happy with me. Zaidy is turning 70 tonight and I will be missing his party. Mommy made a soup with 70 carrots. They asked me what kind of screwed-up priorities do I have to miss Zaidy's party.

If they only knew.

I am doing something far more important than babysitting. I am going to try to save my friend Chedva, and myself. A few months ago I began to plan to leave on my own. Tatty guessed my plans.

"Don't even think about going back to Israel. If you try anything like that I will come right after you and bring you home."

That, I think, is actually a good plan. I know I can't help Chedva on my own. I will run away to Israel and Tatty will come after me and save Chedva. After all, he told me he could help her.

I start looking into tickets. I have a job. I have a passport. I have a bank account. As far as I am concerned, I am over 18 and I figure the decision is mine. At the same time, I don't want to openly defy my parents or cause them worry. And it is clear they are worried about me. Still, this is a case of *pikuach nefesh* - a life at risk. I cannot stand by and let Chedva kill herself because of me. I had made a promise.

Tatty and Mommy ask questions and I answer vaguely. It is not really a secret that I am planning to leave and I do not want to lie. Tatty stops me one day before we leave work and asks to speak to me in an empty office in the school.

I can feel his tension, but I could not have guessed what would happen next.

Tatty asks me point blank if I am planning to go back to Israel.

I answer honestly, "Yes."

Without saying a word, he picks up the phone and dials. I listen in dismay as he says, "Mommy, go into Genendy's room and take her passport and bank book." He does not look at me. "Put them somewhere safe."

He hangs up and looks at me, blinking. "I will not return your passport unless you promise me you won't leave."

I feel an iron chain tighten around my chest - a heavy chain of guilt, fear and rage. I cannot take a deep breath. I cannot scream or cry. My father has taken all of my choices away.

I follow Tatty silently to the car. In complete silence, we drive home. I go up to my room and close the door.

A surge of rage and terror rushes through me as my thoughts become clearer.

If I don't go back to Israel I will kill myself.

I will go up to the roof and jump. I will do it now. I cannot live at home. There is a reason I have been living in Israel. Home is a prison I cannot tolerate.

Tonight I promise Tatty I will not leave. I have no intention of keeping my promise - for myself as much as for Chedva.

I do not really want to die. I am overwhelmed with fear and guilt, and I am also very angry.

Tatty turned me into a liar. But what choice do I have? I cannot take the chance on Chedva's life. Chedva holds me responsible for my promise and so do I.

I stop depositing my paycheck in the bank. I start saving up cash, hiding it between the pages of a book in my room. Tatty waits to give me back my passport. After a month, I ask him where it is. He tells me he gave it to his brother for safekeeping, and would get it back to me soon.

"You aren't planning on using it, are you?"

"No," I lie. "I promised you I wouldn't. Have I ever broken a promise to you?"

"No."

Yet, he hesitates.

I smile reassuringly, hating myself. "You can trust me."

Desperation keeps me from gagging on my words.

I wait patiently, not wanting to stir up suspicion. In the meantime, I make careful plans. It takes Tatty another month to reluctantly give my passport back.

"I'm trusting you," he says, tightening the chain of guilt around my heart.

A few days after getting my passport back, I walk resolutely through the backyard, my mind racing. I really think I'm doing the right thing. I was not given a choice.

I pick up my maroon handbag that I hid in the shed - that same shed with the hole in the roof where I smashed with my foot, hoping I would fall off and break my foot again. That same backyard where I played countless games of softball. I push through shrubs surrounding our property and cut through the grounds of the apartment house next door. I walk down the street and around the corner. There is the taxi I ordered this morning, waiting in front of the house whose address I had randomly chosen.

I am on my way to the airport.

There is a stopover in Holland. The airport is big, lots of open space. Not many people are here right now at three in the morning. I am grateful that there are upholstered benches in the airport, laid out like beds. I will eat something and lie down. I am hungry but none of the food here is labeled kosher. I buy an apple and an orange.

Then, an El Al security guard comes over to me and asks me to follow him.

My parents must have found some way to arrest me and have me sent back home.

I am taken into a room in the airport. Six guards surround me and begin to question me.

"What is your name?"

"Where are you going?"

"Why do you only have a carry on, if you are traveling overseas?"

Now I understand their suspicion. I am traveling overseas with one small carry on.

That is weird. For a moment, I think of telling them the truth, that I am running away from home. But I'm afraid. I recently turned 18. It's hard to believe I will be treated like a legal adult if I admit I'm running away from home.

I tell them I went home for a short visit until the war ended, and my belongings are in Bnei Brak where I am studying for the year.

They switch to Hebrew to test me. They tell me to answer only in Hebrew. I guess I passed the test because they let me go. Exhausted from the stress of the day, I lie down on a bench and try to sleep.

I am aroused by my name repeatedly called over the loudspeaker. "Genendy please come to the El Al check-in, you have a phone call. Genendy. You have a phone call at the El Al desk."

I knew my parents would catch up with me, but I'm still surprised they found me so quickly. I ignore the announcement.

Fifteen minutes later, through half-closed lids I see a flight attendant approaching me. I can barely keep my eyes open.

"Are you Genendy?"

I nod, groggy.

"Please come with me. Your father is on the phone and he would like to speak with you."

I shake my head. "No thanks. I don't want to talk to him."

"Please," she insists. "He is crying! Just talk to him for a minute and tell him you're okay. He is very worried."

Reluctantly I pull myself to my feet and follow her to the phone. She hands it to me.

I stand there holding it in front of me, staring at it blankly.

The flight attendant motions for me to hold the phone up to my ear.

Right. I slowly put the phone to my ear. Tatty is crying on the other end.

"Genendy! Why are you doing this?"

The rage I can barely contain comes through in my voice. "You don't know?"

"Why are you so angry?" He sounds so sad and puzzled.

I don't bother to answer.

"None of us slept all night. The children are so upset…" Tatty continues.

I say nothing.

"It doesn't matter. Listen to me. I booked a flight and I will be there tomorrow. When you arrive in Israel, my friend Aaron will pick you up. He will take you wherever you want to go. I had to buy business class tickets because that's all that is available on such short notice. I used the money you inherited from great-aunt Sherry to pay for this. I hope you'll forgive me but I had no choice."

Tatty's friend Aaron is divorced. The community shunned him after it was rumored that he abused his wife. I think he lost custody of his children, one of whom is in my grade at school. Tatty invited him to our house, apparently the only one in the community to reach out to him. Aaron became a regular Friday night guest.

He owes a lot to Tatty, and I suspect he will do anything for him.

I have no intention of going with Tatty's friend Aaron anywhere.

At the airport in Israel, I dial the number of Rebbetzin Shlesingman. It is the number that Tatty gave me for a woman, a relative of a friend of his, who can help my friend Chedva. I suddenly realize if no one answers I don't have a plan B. For a moment, I think of going to live on an Israeli kibbutz, changing my name, and disappearing forever.

A woman answers the phone and I ask her if she is Mrs. Shlesingman. She is. I tell her I am in the airport and I came from America to speak with her, to try to help my friend in Bnei Brak. She sounds taken aback. She asks me if I have friends or relatives in Israel. I say yes. She tells me to come see her the next morning at her home in the Jewish quarter of the Old City.

Tatty's friend Aaron, a huge man of six four, is standing outside the airport waiting for me as promised. I try to ignore him but he walks over.

For a moment, I wonder if he is planning to grab me, force me into his car, and keep me prisoner until Tatty gets here.

But he gives me a friendly smile.

"Do you need a ride somewhere?"

I am wary, but physically and emotionally too exhausted to fight my parents right now.

"How do I know you don't have something hidden up your sleeve?" I ask.

He rolls up his jacket sleeves and shakes his arms. "Nope. Nothing there. I'm just the chauffeur. I'll take you wherever you want to go."

"Will you take me to Bnei Brak?"

"Sure." I follow him to the car, suddenly grateful that my parents have everything under control and are taking care of me from a distance. I ask Aaron to drop me at the apartment of my friend Shani who is learning in Bais Yaakov Bnei Brak this year. Shani is sharing the apartment with a few other American girls, all studying at the same school this post-high school year.

Aaron hands me a paper with a phone number.

"If you need somewhere to sleep tonight I have cousins here in Bnei Brak who would be happy to have you over. They won't bother you or ask you any questions. Don't hesitate to call me if you need anything." I nod and watch him drive away.

Shani seems shocked and nervous when I tell her I ran away from home.

I ask her if I can sleep in her apartment for the night. She calls her counselor to ask for permission.

No I can't. I don't think she wants me here, anyway. My running away disturbs her.

I accomplished my mission of getting Tatty to come to Israel, and I'm out of options. I call Aaron and he takes me to his cousin's house for the night. The house is nicer than any I have seen so far in Israel. My relatives in Jerusalem and Bnei Brak are poverty-stricken compared to this luxury. I am shown to a nice bedroom with matching built-in furniture. No one asks me any questions. Aaron tells me Tatty is arriving the next day and they will pick me up together.

Exhausted, I fall asleep quickly.

The next morning, Tatty hugs me with tears in his eyes. "Don't worry. I'm not angry," he says. I feel numb. I don't say anything.

Aaron lives by himself. He has cockroaches in his apartment and warns us about them. He says they don't bother him because he eats lots of garlic. We share the spare bedroom. Tatty tells me all the children were upset and crying when he left. My sister Devorah who is 14 wouldn't go to school and couldn't sleep. He tells me I don't have to answer him, but the only reason he can think of that I would run away and hurt my siblings like this is because I have a sexual relationship with Chedva. He tells me I don't have to answer and not to worry. He will get me the help I need.

It takes me a few minutes to digest what Tatty is saying. When it finally registers, my brain and body freeze, horrified.

I try to never let anyone touch me. I wouldn't even get undressed in the same room with Chedva or even my own sisters. Yet, I feel so ashamed. I thought Tatty knew me best. Tatty must know what he is talking about. Tatty promises that if I come back home with him he will take me to see his friend, a psychologist, who owes him a favor.

Tatty is very persuasive. Reluctantly, I agree to go home with him. We will spend Shabbos in Israel and leave on Sunday.

PART 3:

REMEMBERING

"Those who cannot remember the past are condemned to repeat it."
George Santayana

My first therapist

Yeshiva college resembles a university campus. It has sprawling brick buildings, basketball courts, and staff family homes, located a 12-minute drive from the rest of the Orthodox community. The families of the teachers and staff who live on campus have on average six to ten children. The *yeshiva* has a high school and religious learning program, and attracts students who want a religious experience along with a college degree. At night the students attend a nearby Christian college to get a degree. There are crosses on the walls, but the school is accepting and accommodating to the *yeshiva* schedule, so rabbinic permission is given.

My father's only brother, Nachi, teaches ninth grade in the high school and lives with his wife and seven children on the campus. Visiting the *yeshiva* campus is like stepping into an alternative Jewish world. I am always rather jealous of my cousins. The children living on the *yeshiva* campus are very close and, as my mother describes it, "run in packs." My cousins are closer to their friends on the campus than they are to us. They seem to have few rules and nothing to fear as all of their neighbors are religious and know and love them. They can walk around the campus at night without concern and spend huge blocks of time at friends' homes without anyone worrying as to their whereabouts. They seem to know they are special and had a bond that the rest of us children in the community could never hope to develop. When we spend *Shabbos* on *yeshiva* campus, I feel like an outsider.

My first therapist, Dr. Davids, is the daughter of the *rosh yeshiva*, the head-master, and lives on the *yeshiva* campus with her family. It is unusual for a *rosh yeshiva*'s daughter to go to college and get a degree in psychology. My family looks at college and anything to do with it with distrust. How can one stay true to Torah values in a secular college environment? My mother supposes that Dr. Davids would come home from her classes and run everything she learned by her father, the *rosh yeshiva,* and he would let her know what she could believe and what she could not. The Orthodox community needs a trained therapist and she, for some reason, is chosen. My cousins who live on the *yeshiva* campus are close with Dr. Davids, her family and children. My parents are friends of the family. My father had helped her counsel couples in distress and told me that she agreed to see me as a favor to him. She would charge him very little as he had helped her with one of her children in the past.

I think nothing of this. My father is well connected and known in the community for his involvement with difficult children. Finally, someone is taking my need for help seriously, but I am overwhelmed with trepidation.

Dr. Davids' office is located on a quiet side street in a new town house. Everything smells new. Her office is one flight up and through a small waiting area. We sit in comfortable armchairs facing each other. I often focus on the white blinds behind her as we speak.

Dr. Davids tells me she usually doesn't see her friends' children on principle, but she made an exception in my case because she has so much respect for my father. Dr. Davids says she is not the kind of therapist who goes into people's past or asks about their toilet training, for example. She is very goal-oriented.

I want very much to trust Dr. Davids and I try to be as honest with her as I can. I have no clue what therapy entails. I assumed she would see me for a number of hours at a time over the course of a few days and help me sort out my problems. I am shocked and disturbed to find that after meeting for about 45 minutes she interrupts me.

"Well, we have to end for today. I'll try to schedule a time in for you next week. I'll be in touch."

I am clueless. The idea of therapeutic boundaries is a brand-new concept, as is therapy. All I know is that Tatty's friend, Dr. Davids, is supposed to fix me. When I don't feel fixed, I believe that it's my fault.

I see Dr. Davids about once a week for eight months. We never have a regular appointment time, and I am not really sure what I should be talking to her about. It is all very unclear and makes me less confident in myself, not more.

When I finally summon the courage to ask her if it could be possible that I had an emotionally sexual relationship with Chedva (I know it wasn't physical), she laughs at me. She says there is no such thing. I am so embarrassed. Dr. Davids encourages me to consider the option of leaving home and moving to New York to live in an apartment with other young women my age. I cannot imagine doing such a thing. We talk a lot about depression and make a list of goals for the next six months, year, and five years.

I leave my sessions dazed, not knowing when Dr. Davids will have the time to put me into her busy schedule again.

Once again, I spend most of my day in bed. Tatty is certain that I am falling apart. He spends time with me, trying to help me. We go for walks and he takes me on his errands so we can talk. I don't talk much. So Tatty talks instead. I am Tatty's confidante. Tatty is concerned that Mommy's difficult pregnancy is actually a molar like *her* mother had.

He continues to talk to me as if I am his intimate friend. He tells me as we walk together that he is depressed and he wants to discuss the problem he is experiencing with our rabbinic leaders, the *gedolim*. The *gedolim*, he tells me, are not supporting Zaidy in his attempt to destroy my uncle Avi who my family believes to be a child molester. The *gedolim*, in Tatty's opinion, were clearly making an error. He also confides in me, on one of our walks, that he cannot understand why a parent is gossiping about him because he hit her child in the face and broke his glasses. This parent gave him permission to hit her child, after all, he says. We walk some more, and he shares his shock that old friends of his are getting a divorce because of an affair in the marriage. We get back home, and I am going to get ready for bed. Tatty wants me to know that he is completely sat-isfied with his relationship with Mommy in *every* way. I listen and then get into bed, too depressed to move. Something feels wrong, but I do not have words to explain what I am feeling. Tatty needs just as much support as I do, but I do not know what to do with that knowledge, and it feels too much for me to hold.

The next time Tatty comes into my room and offers to take me for a ride, I decline. He expresses concern about my not eating enough. He says I am losing too much weight. He threatens to start weighing me every day.

I actually am starving myself on purpose. It is the only thing in my life I have any control over. It helps keep my awful, overwhelming feelings in check. I make strict rules for myself to follow. I can have one protein, one carb a day. The rest of my food is fruits and veggies. If I break the rules, I don't eat for the rest of the day. Then I get so hungry it's hard to control myself and not binge on sugar and carbs. I am stuck in a vicious cycle.

I have a sudden moment of clarity. Or, maybe it is desperation. I really need a parent right now. I hear myself saying to Tatty, "I am your *daugh-ter*. I'm *not* your wife. I'm *not* your rabbi. I'm *not* your therapist. It's not appropriate for you to talk to me about your problems. If you want to talk to someone about your problems talk to your wife, your rabbi, your therapist about it, not to me."

Tatty is taken aback. His eyebrows nearly join mid-brow.

"I don't understand. Isn't communication a two-way street?"

"No, it's not."

Tatty walks out of my room, clearly hurt. I can't believe I actually said that. But I am beyond caring. I need a real parent. It is becoming clear to me that my parents cannot offer me what I need. I know that something is very wrong inside, and it is a lot more than having parents who don't get me, as Dr. Davids says.

Trying to trust myself

I need to see photos of myself as a young child. Maybe pictures will help explain what I need to know. I need to know if a little girl named Genendy ever really existed. Because I don't feel real. And I don't feel like I was her. Who was I? Who am I?

Photos are the closest proof I have. I ask Mommy for the family photo box (a hat box) which she keeps in her closet. She does not want me to see the photos.

"Why not?" I ask.

"I'm worried that you'll take pictures without permission."

I hadn't thought of taking pictures. "I promise that if I want a picture, I will ask permission before taking it."

"No."

There is something bad about me that they, my parents, must know, but they are on a mission to keep me from knowing. Even more than that, they are on a mission to rid me of whatever it is that is so bad about me, without me ever finding out. I go to my parents' closet and get out the photo box myself and take it up to my room. A few minutes later Tatty comes pounding up the stairs.

"Give me the box. Now."

"No," I say calmly. "There is no reason I shouldn't be able to see pictures of myself when I was little." He blinks. "Give me the box."

I am trying to hide my fear. Tatty is hiding his fear too.

"What are you, Mommy's policeman? If she has a problem with me seeing pictures of myself as a child let her come up and discuss it with me herself." That upsets him.

"I'm shocked that you would speak to me this way. I'm your father! How could you talk to your father this way?" I am shocked too.

This is becoming a new habit. I have always gone out of my way not to upset Tatty before.

Now, I am too angry and too hurt to care. But I give back the box. And I am scared. Because after 19 years of submission I am openly disobeying both of my parents. My parents who are not behaving like parents. It seems they are as scared of me as I am of myself. It seems they are trying to protect me and themselves from me. What is so scary and bad about me that I can't even be allowed to see photos of myself as a child? Is it because I ran away from home? The distrust began when I was very young, so that can't be it.

What could it possibly be?!

I am confused. I do not know who to trust. My father? Dr. Davids? Myself?

After a few months of therapy, I am surprised when Dr. Davids asks me to ask my mother what it was like toilet training me. My feelings and acting -out behaviors are becoming more intense. Dr. Davids tells me that I'm spinning my wheels. I wish she would adopt me and take me home with her, but I am an adult and I know she won't. I have to get away and I'm starting to feel desperate. Dr. Davids insists that in conjunction with my sessions with her, I see her colleague, an art therapist in the office across the waiting room from her own.

She also tells me that she thinks I have been sexually abused and repressed it. She presses me about my uncle Avi who is on trial for molesting his own children, and who I know I spent time with as a young child after he married my aunt Leah. I have no memories of him molesting me, though. Dr. Davids seems frustrated with me. She tells me unless I see her colleague, the art therapist in the same office, she can't treat me anymore. I go to the art therapy, and then at home I draw horrible pictures of the parts inside my mind and what happened to them. But I don't show them to my art therapist or to Dr. Davids.

I tell Tatty on one of our drives – they are getting less frequent because it is getting difficult for me to be around him – that Dr. Davids thinks I was sexually abused as a child and repressed it. Tatty, after a few moments of silence, agrees that, yes, it would make a lot of sense. Neither one of us suggests or even hints that one of the people who abused me is him. Tatty tells me that getting married would solve a lot of my issues. He encourages me to start dating. I look at him silently, incredulous. Is he really this clueless?

I am thinking a lot about my early childhood and remembering Zaidy exposing himself to me and Hadassa in the bathroom on the third floor of *yeshiva*. I have other memories about his bedroom on the same floor in *yeshiva*. A terror so strong surrounds these memories, my mind won't allow entry. I cannot go into that room and survive. I remember that Zaidy moved out of *yeshiva* when I was very little. He bought a small white house around the corner. My mother told me she and her siblings wanted him to have his own space. But the *yeshiva* was full of empty rooms and empty space. Why did they want him to move out?

I am reading *The Courage to Heal*, a book about sexual abuse, and the issues are all so very familiar to me. I can relate to the stories from other survivors in so many different ways. According to this book, exposing yourself to a child is a sexual violation. I sense there were other violations by Zaidy. My mind does not want to go there. Pain. Fear. Confusion. I felt so uncomfortable around him. Why did he walk around in front of me in only his thin white boxers and *tzitzis*? The thought of him makes me shiver. He sexually abused me. I know he did. And it wasn't just him. There were others involved.

The quake

It is a warm summer night. I have been in therapy for six months, since I ran away from home. My youngest sister, Elisheva, five years old, is crying quietly in her bed.

I go to her, to try to comfort her. She is wearing only her panties.

I ask her why she is crying. At first, she doesn't answer. I ask if someone hurt her feelings and she nods. I go through the list of our siblings. She shakes her head. No. It wasn't a brother or sister who hurt her feelings.

"Did Mommy hurt your feelings?"

A nod. Yes.

"Does Mommy know that she hurt your feelings?"

No.

"Do you want me to hold you?"

Yes.

I pull her on to my lap and hug her. I tell her that she is a good little girl and it isn't her fault that my mother doesn't know she was crying and that she had hurt her feelings.

Suddenly my mother is calling from the bottom of the stairs.

There is fear in her voice.

"Genendy, what are you doing? Leave Elisheva alone."

She doesn't trust me with my little sister.

I am holding a little girl in panties.

Almost naked.

I feel as if I have been caught red-handed molesting a child.

I leave my little sister and crawl into bed wrapped in a hot blanket of shame.

My heart is thumping.

I am bad. Very bad. My mother knows. She always has.

I turn my head and bricks crash down around me.

I can see a spot behind me that until this moment was always blocked from view. I always knew it was there but I couldn't see past the bricks of dissociation.

I am very small.

I know what I am about to see and I don't want to look.

I can't look.

At the same time, I can't look away.

He did hurt you.

He hurt you in your room at night.

Not just once.

Crash!

Many times.

Crash!

Something is in my mouth cutting off my breath. I'm going to die.

I am not real. This can't be real. I must be imagining this.

Crash!

You know this is true.

You have always known about this.

You just never had words for it before.

I see myself lying in bed in my room that I share with my sisters in our little white stucco house. I am feeling familiar feelings of terror and shame.

I am trapped.

My father comes into my room and lies on my bed.

I stare at the red and white checkered curtains.

A familiar numbness creeps into my mind.

I am not real. I can't be.

He rolls partially on top of me. I can't breathe. I can't move. Something is poking at me. Cutting me. He's too heavy. I am going to die. I want to die. I have to die.

Then, I am back in my bedroom in the present.

I am shaking and I can't move. I'm in shock.

Words, as if writing themselves, scrawl in horror across my mind.

Tatty raped me.

It was Tatty.

Tatty raped me when I was little.

I don't believe it.

Not my father.

It can't be. Not Tatty.

Anyone else but Tatty.

I force myself to look again and there is no mistaking him.

I don't want to see this.

I don't want to know this.

My uncle Avi I could accept.

Zaidy too.

But not Tatty.

I need Tatty.

I order my brain to take back the images.

I must have made this up.

My mind is playing tricks on me.

My mind replays the scene over and over. An inner voice says, "You always knew. You just didn't turn your head far enough to see."

I float near my body.

My arms and head tingle. I somehow manage to get myself out of bed and downstairs to the bathroom. Leaning against the sink I peer at myself in the mirror. I am wavering, reeling. My image in the mirror is fluid. My legs are shaking. I can barely hold on to the sink. I reach up slowly to touch my face and make sure I am still here. A white face fades in and out of focus. I slap my cheek hard. Is that my face? Am I real? Is this real? What is wrong with me? Why on earth am I thinking and remembering this?

I don't believe this.

It's a mistake.

Tatty, no! Don't hurt me!

More bricks crash down beside me.

Bruising.

He did hurt you.

He hurt you in your room at night.

Not just once.

Crash!

NOOOOOOOOOOOOOO!! Tatty!!

Tatty, I need you!

Take this away. God take this away, please!

I float around the house in shock. I am aware that I am hearing my voice from a distance.

I am not real.

This is not real.

Tatty wouldn't have done that.

Never.

I must have made it up.

I must be crazy.

I hope I am.

I must pray for help.

Please God, don't let me remember things that aren't true! Please let me only remember things that really happened. Don't do this to me, God. Please, God. I want to know the truth! I don't want to remember, or think, that Tatty raped me if it isn't true. This is way over my head. I can't do this alone. God, I am desperate! Help me!! I don't want this!!!

I thought I knew some things about myself
then the quake began
a faint tremor that rose to
this mind-cracking crescendo
shaking me to the core
reality split me down the middle
tearing the facts from my white-knuckled grasp
hurling me into a black abyss of
nothing to hold on to
here I crouch in my corner of cold illusion
fatigued fingers stirring painful circles
in a sizzling boiling cauldron
of tears.

Grasping for help

I am just beginning to get an inkling of the difficulties I will end up facing in the coming years. Flashbacks and panic attacks are an everyday occurrence. I feel like I jumped off a cliff believing my family would catch me, and I am finding only empty air.

I am crash landing, a hard and painful landing that is shattering every part of my identity, my safe world, and my reality. Even as I gasp for air to breathe, even as I realize that my life as I thought it was had never really existed in the first place, I know and believe deep down that God has a good reason for all of this, and that he will help me survive somehow, and eventually I will be okay.

As I write the following poem, I ponder the irony of me, writing a poem. I have never been a poetry person. I don't like or read poetry. I don't really know where my poems are coming from. My only explanation is that my *neshama* (soul), or a very wise part of me, is writing them to me. Once again I discover an inner resource of strength and creativity to help myself deal with the impossible. I am proud when *Life's Tools* is published in a local Jewish publication.

Life's Tools

Heavy metal tools
    tumble down on me
    I reach out to catch them
    as they fall
    I grasp them tightly
    but I don't know why
    the unbearable strain
    on my arms and chest
    tell me to drop them
    they are too heavy
    but I won't let them go
    and I feel myself
    falling... falling
    then darkness and despair
    overcome me
    Awakening...
    I find I did not let go
    the tools are embedded
    in my tightly clenched fists
    slowly carefully
    I stand up
    slowly... slowly
    I learn to move with them
    and slowly

as my wounds heal
my muscles become accustomed to their weight
until I do not feel
their heaviness
only their security
I am stronger
I am better armed
I will keep these tools
they are mine for life
I did not drop them
I could not drop them
God sent them my way
because He knows I will need them
to build.

Dr. Davids assures me that what I say in the office is confidential and that she will not be speaking with my parents.

After the memory of Tatty hurting me, I start contemplating suicide. I tell Dr. Davids I am having thoughts but I have no plans to act on them.

She tells my parents.

For the first time in my life I hear my mother tell me, "I love you." First, she begs me not to kill myself. Then she tells me she loves me.

Does she only know how to love me if she thinks I might be dead?

Dr. Davids tries to convince me to speak to my mother, to tell her what I am remembering, what is so badly upsetting me, but I can't. I am protecting our relationship, protecting my parents' relationship with her, protecting myself from what I correctly sense will be her denial. She tells me I am delaying gratification, and I should just tell her. Her ideas confuse me. I don't think it will be gratifying to know what I know or to share this with her.

Our house is so clean
its rooms echo purity

wandering through
open doors and
empty spaces
I wonder how my hands became stained
amid such perfect cleanliness
the attic and basement leave no clue
the closets speak generations of praise
in confused disbelief
I begin the insane task of
digging under the basement floor
insane
muscles bruised and aching
years of frustration
and then
buried under layers
of pure innocent earth
I come upon a well of filth
that perfectly matches the stains
on my soul

Tatty tells me that Rabbi Tambor, an internationally known and respected rabbi who wrote the book on self-esteem that he and my mother recently gave me, is in town. Tatty says if I really want to I can meet with him. I am excited by the idea. I know I need help. I need guidance. I really liked his book.

The rabbi agrees to meet with me after a parlor meeting in someone's home. This is the first time I am reaching out to a rabbi and I am afraid to hope, and also afraid not to hope. What can he tell me?

Rabbi Tambor looks tired. He wears a black hat and long black coat. His beard is graying. I can tell he can't give me much time. He asks me what I do and I tell him that I'm a pre-school teacher. He asks me my age. I tell him I just turned 19. He asks me how he can help me. I haltingly explain that I need guidance. I tell him I have memories of my grandfather molesting me. I do not tell him about Tatty. I am not ready to begin dealing with my father. I look at him to see if he believes me. He nods.

"I believe you," he says. Wow. He believes me? This seems too easy.

My grandfather was a *rosh yeshiva*. "A *talmid chacham*," I explain. "A brilliant scholar. I don't know how to deal with these memories. I don't know what to do."

"What is your grandfather's name?" Rabbi Tambor asks.

I tell him. His eyes widen, and his head and upper body move slightly forward in his chair. He gives me an intense look. "It didn't happen," he says quickly. "It was your imagination. You're young. Get married and move on with your life." I ask him if he thinks other people should know about my memories. "No. Don't talk about it. Forget about it."

My head jerks ever so slightly as if absorbing a blow. Then a numbness fills my head. I thank the rabbi for his time and stumble outside to the car where Tatty is waiting for me, trying to process what just happened. *Slap! A punch in the head! Ouch!* How could he say he believed me and then totally backpedal when he heard Zaidy's name? He must know him or know his reputation. His reaction makes no sense.

I send Rabbi Tambor a letter a few days later telling him that I am very disturbed by my meeting with him, and what he said to me. I tell him I felt slapped after my talk with him. I ask him how he could say what he did to me. How could he tell me it never happened, and to forget about it and not talk about it? I tell him I wish I could forget about it but I can't. I need to talk about my memories in order to try to make sense of them and heal. Rabbi Tambor writes me back saying he didn't mean it. He writes that he was very tired when he spoke to me. He says I should certainly talk to my therapist about it… just not to anyone else. And he wishes me luck.

There is a woman whose books I am reading and learning a lot from. Her name is Miriam Adahan. She writes about mental and emotional abuse and how abusers' minds work. Some of her descriptions help me make sense of my parents. Tatty tells me that Miriam is a well-known speaker.

Her nephew is in his class, and she is another person I might want to speak to, to get some *chizuk* (strength) from.

I arrange a meeting with her. I know I am taking a risk.

I tell her about Zaidy and Tatty. I am afraid to tell, but I need guidance and Rabbi Tambor was no help. I am determined to find help. I know I can't survive this alone.

Miriam is very approachable. She tells me with clarity and calm that she believes me. Even when I tell her that no one else does, and Rabbi Tambor said it was my imagination.

"They will deny, rationalize, minimize and ignore abuse," she says. "That is the reality. The only way to fight it and to win is by healing yourself. You can't change abusers or deniers."

Miriam invites me to a workshop she is giving in a few days. She thinks it will help me cope.

I am the youngest one at the workshop by far. Miriam has us write down our biggest challenges. Then she has us switch hands and, using our non-dominant hand, write from our soul the reason we have these challenges and what we are supposed to do with them.

I feel kind of light-headed. I wonder if I'm going to pass out and I put my head down on the table for a few minutes until the panic passes and my breathing slows. This is hard. I write about my memories about Tatty and Zaidy in tiny letters, hoping no one will see. I cover the page with my arm. I write about how there is no way anyone in my family will believe me. I am afraid to switch hands because I think maybe I am being punished for something really bad… and the truth is about to be told. I switch hands and a few simple words come from my pencil as if on their own.

You are supposed to heal and use this experience to help other people.

I look at the words I just wrote, not really comprehending them. I cannot even help myself, how can I hope to help others? But inside, deep in my soul there stirs a clarity and purpose. And hope.

Betrayal

I do not feel safe sleeping at home anymore. One night I call Dr. Davids on my way to a motel. I had slept in a local motel the night before as well. I tell her I just had to get away from home. Nothing feels safe there. She has Tatty bring me over to her house to sleep.

The experience of coming into Dr. Davids' home, her personal space, and watching her tell her six-year-old that she thinks she needs a hug and kiss, and then hug and kiss her daughter the next morning, is confusing and painful. No one ever told me they thought I needed a hug and a kiss. The idea of someone telling me they think they need to hug and kiss me is novel and incredible, and also makes me feel slightly nauseous. I don't think I could allow someone that close, even though a part of me craves physical affection so badly my skin hurts.

The boundaries in our relationship, which were unclear and unreliable to me from the outset, continue to blur. My parents insist on speaking to Dr. Davids by phone. They tell her that I always have to have my own way, and Dr. Davids seems to agree that I am a control freak. My parents convince me that they should meet with Dr. Davids and she convinces me to give her permission. But then I realize that if my parents meet with her, it will end my relationship with her, so I change my mind and tell Dr. Davids that I do not give permission. Dr. Davids would have none of that. She tells me I am jerking her around, and she will meet with my parents without my consent.

Well, I decide that if my parents are going to see Dr. Davids, I am going along. Maybe it is desperation to hang on to some sense of control over my therapy. My parents refuse to bring me. I keep insisting and finally they say I can come, as long as I agree to stay in the car until they call me in. I agree. My parents leave me in the car while they go inside to meet with my therapist.

Sitting in that car alone, a rage builds and bangs around inside my ribs, trapped in my chest with nowhere to go. This is so wrong! I am 19! How can they do this? How can they treat me like a child and take over my therapy? I have to do something. I get out of the car and quickly climb the stairs to Dr. Davids' office, telling myself I will wait in the waiting room. I sit in the waiting room, my outrage growing by the second, listening to my parents and my therapist discussing me without my consent in the next room. Finally, I can contain myself no longer. I open the door, walk in, sit down and announce, "This is my life. I have a right to be here."

The three of them stare at me in shocked silence. Dr. Davids finally breaks the silence by saying that there is something going on here that she hadn't imagined. She suggests we end the session and regroup at a later date. The ride home is strained and silent.

I sit with the guilt of knowing that once again I have let my parents down. At my next meeting with Dr. Davids she tells me that there are serious boundary issues in my family that she hadn't been aware of. She also tells me that I have been keeping something from her that she doesn't want to know, and that she is sending me to another therapist.

The last thread of trust is shattered. To describe this experience with Dr. Davids as damaging is an understatement. I was counting on her to help me, and not only does she fail to help me, she is hurting me and abandoning me. I feel confused by her divided loyalties, and my own divided loyalties to myself and my parents, and by what feels like a betrayal by Dr. Davids.

I decide to write to her, trying to explain the pain, and trying to hold on to my sanity and my sense of reality.

Dear Dr. Davids,

> *I am troubled by feelings of anger and hate for what you did to me. I feel that the reason you initially agreed to see me professionally was primarily as a favor to my father. I think the boundaries were fuzzy from the beginning.*

> *How was I supposed to work through what I needed to when my father is the one who abused me, and you obviously respected him very much? I can recall trying to talk about the anger I had for my parents and you saying, "But I can tell you really respect them a lot!"*

The main issues I needed to work on in therapy were trust and boundaries. Why did you let me sleep at your house? Were you trying to "rescue" me? I don't think it is appropriate for a therapist to have a client sleep over, especially when the client has boundary issues. When I asked you not to meet with my parents, you said that they and you had a right to meet, and you felt like I was trying to push you around. You said that I always have to have things my way...

You broke confidentiality by meeting with my parents without my consent. I was your client, and over 18. I don't know if you realize but legally and professionally you were way out of line. I could sue you for meeting with them without my consent.

You seemed to think that I was the one out of line for crashing your little meeting.

How could I trust you, knowing that you would meet with my parents when I clearly asked you not to? I think it was irresponsible and inappropriate for you to agree to work with me in the first place. When a child runs away from home there are obviously conflicts with the parents. Knowing my parents beforehand should have alerted you to obvious boundary issues. You should have referred me to someone else immediately.

You were pushing me pretty quickly to the edge. I almost killed myself because of you.

I cannot watch you daven on Yom Kippur, hating you and thinking about how you messed up my life and hurt me very badly, and you don't even seem to be aware of it.

Genendy

I did not receive a response, but I am not one to give up easily. I write her again, and to this day, I have not received a response.

PART 4:

TELLING

Tatty

I speak to my sister Gittel. She is the first one in the family I tell. I tell her that I remember Tatty raping me when I was little. I am 20 years old and Gittel is 23. We work together. She is the teacher and I am her assistant. I admire and learn from her how to manage a classroom. She seems to like and care for me. Maybe, just maybe, I have an ally. Gittel looks shocked at my disclosure, but she says that she'll always be there for me. She says that what was done to me is not my responsibility. She says a lot of things, but I don't feel like she's really there. I feel dirty. I am so scared. I don't know where I am. It feels like it was wrong to tell her, like she'll do something awful with this information. I don't know what to do. I feel exposed. Naked. Helpless. I hate myself. I feel like I shouldn't exist. I don't know why.

I try to talk to her about it again a second time, to explain my guilt. She tells me after thinking it over she decided I must be mistaken. Tatty would never have done those things to me. It couldn't have happened. I hope she is right. *Then, why do I remember him hurting me?* God help me see the truth. I just have to know the truth.

Show me the right way to deal with this.

Gittel must have said something to Tatty because he takes me for one of his famous walks. Tatty tells me I am heading down a dangerous path, and that no one but him really loves me. He tells me I have to stop seeing Dr. Cohen, the new therapist Dr. Davids sent me to, because Dr. Cohen is convincing me of things that never happened. He is planning to sue her in Bais Din. I am confused. Dr. Cohen didn't convince me of anything. And Dr. Davids made it clear that she doesn't want to know the truth. I am so alone. Gone and alone. Dr. Cohen recently introduced me to the concept of having a younger self, an inner child inside me. I definitely have that. And that younger part of me knows exactly what happened to her.

What does Tatty want from me? He wants me to love him. He's scared. I can't get in touch with myself. I don't feel anything. Just a vague sense of shame and guilt. It's very distant and vague. I'm not really feeling it. I just sense it. I can't stay home anymore. I have no place to go. Nothing. No feelings. I don't exist right now. I can't write anymore. There is nothing to write about because nothing is here. I'm not here. This is weird. I feel gone. That's all. Just gone. And I can't stop thinking about Tatty's hands.

My skin prickles and my stomach tightens when I think of his hands. I was very little when they undressed me and touched me all over. Gently at first, fondling my body, my chest, my stomach, then downward to private parts that should not be touched. It felt weird. I was afraid to move. I felt so dirty and icky. I was terrified. I wanted to scream but I couldn't move my mouth. He stuck something in me. It felt like a sharp, hard pressure and I couldn't take it. I couldn't breathe. I tried to scream. I retched and gagged but nothing came up. Then I passed out. It still hurts now, like something tore apart inside.

I hate him. I want to kill him. I feel so violated and worthless and humiliated. Like a piece of dirt. He had no right to do that. But it must have been my fault. There must have been something gross about my body that made him do that to me. I know I'll never feel normal inside. Sometimes I want to be dead. I can't even remember where this happened, or when exactly. But I feel it happening over and over. I remember things. His hands. The pain. Was it my imagination? If it is, I think I'll kill myself. What a dirty mind that could think up such things! What filth! Will I ever know the truth? Do I want to? Ouch. It still hurts. Will I ever be able to have children?

What's wrong with me? What really happened?

Gittel and Tatty must be right. I can't believe that my father could have hurt me like that. It must be something else that brought up those images and feelings.

My younger part, the part causing all this trouble, says he lay on me, kissed me, touched my private parts.

I hate her!! Why is she telling me these things? She is so sad and lonely. She is in so much pain I don't know what to do. Don't do that Ta! Don't hurt me. I hate you!! I want to kill you!

What did you do to me?? I want to die. I can't feel so awful all the time.

Go away, Ta, don't touch me! I hate his hands! Get off me! Get away from me! Don't hurt me! Hold me! Love me!

I'll kill myself. I can't deal with this. I'll choke you until you suffocate!

I'm so angry at myself for having these memories. I'm all alone. No one will help me. I can't stop crying.

Ma, why aren't you helping me?

I can't be around Tatty.

Since he found out about the memories I have about him, it's worse. I can't be around my mother either, but it's not as bad. I hate being around my brother Shalom. I don't know why but I feel violated. Can't stand him. Hadassa too. Something about her is gross and disgusting and hateful to the younger part of me.

The rest of my siblings, I have no problems with. I love them. I want to be around them. They will be sad if I leave. So will I. What to do? I feel like crying. I hurt so badly inside.

Searing pain cuts through my body, from all the memories and years of being alone, locked up inside myself, trying to ignore the hurt and loneliness. It is the pain of not having parents to turn to, or friends and teachers to care about me, an engulfing sadness and shame is twisting my insides. I taught the tears to turn around in my eyes and slide backwards into my stomach. There was no one to see them anyway. Now years and years of tears are coming up. I am bent over in pain clutching my stomach as I let some of them out. Crying. Rocking. Alone. Terrible, empty aloneness.

No one can see this shame-filled pain. I'm burning and burning. She is not me, but she is there and she is real. No one heard. She was bleeding because she was too small. Tatty had to cut her because she was very little. The sharpness, pain, bruises, badness feel like they are still inside me. It doesn't feel safe at home anymore, but I have nowhere to go.

Every night since my father spoke to me, I wake up at about two in the morning. I toss and turn for a few hours, and then fall back to sleep for an hour or so. I wake up shaking with an empty feeling inside. I sense that something is very wrong even before I remember what it is. Then it hits me. *I shouldn't be here. Tatty knows. What if he's innocent?*

But he can't be. He's not. If he is innocent, I wouldn't be remembering these things. God wouldn't do that to me. I must trust myself and my younger part. But how can I?

I need my therapist to believe me, and then I can believe myself. I think I will keep reliving these memories until I can say to the younger part of me: *Yes, I know this happened. I believe you. It's awful for you.*

My new therapist, Dr. Cohen, tells me that most likely I will come to an understanding of what happened over time, as I work through the memories in therapy, but that it is also possible I may never know the whole truth.

Still, I don't believe my younger self, so she keeps on throwing the evidence at me. The feelings and memories. But I can't validate them. Maybe because my therapist can't. So when I'm having an attack, a flashback, and my younger self is yelling at me, *"Can't you see what he's doing to me?!"* I want to yell back that I do see it, and I do believe it because it feels so real. Instead I yell, "Why are you having these memories if they didn't really happen?! Why are you doing this to me?! Why do you want me to believe that my father did that?!"

And she always answers in gut-wrenching sobs, *"Because he did. Because this really happened to me! Please believe me. Please save me!"*

Moving out

Last night I slept in a cheap motel again. It was scary. I slept with mace under my pillow and pushed all the furniture I could manage to move in front of the door. Staying in a dangerous place feels emotionally, if not physically, safer than staying at home. I don't want to stay at home anymore. I am living in two different realities: my external reality where I don't know what to think about my life, even as I appear to be functioning normally, going to work, showering, eating, sleeping, and my inner world, a young child part of me knows I was raped and molested by my father. Nothing makes sense.

I call Esther.

I met Esther at a support group for religious incest survivors I joined to try to sort things out for myself. Something about Esther reminds me of Dr. Davids. She is the nurturing "mother bear" type, something I never got enough of. I crave being with her. The pain of losing Dr. Davids is soothed when I am with Esther. I am drawn to her strength. Esther doesn't care what anyone thinks of her. She protected her own children from a child molester in her family in spite of intense pressure and denial from relatives. Esther did what she deeply believed was the right thing to do. I tell her that I am moving out of my parents' home.

I ask her for the number of the group therapist. I plan to call the therapist to find out if she knows of a women's shelter I could go to. Esther's reaction is immediate. Without hesitation, she says, "Come live with us. You can share a room with my 12-year-old daughter, Zahava."

I am taken aback.

"How do you know that your daughter will be okay with this? Shouldn't you ask her first?"

"She'll be fine with it," Esther assures me.

"And what about your husband? Shouldn't you ask him first?"

"Meir will be fine with it too. You'll meet him. You'll see."

She is so sure.

What kind of person invites a virtual stranger off the street to come and live with her?

I don't trust this woman. I decide to visit Esther and see what she, her home and family are like before I take her up on an offer to move in. I tell Esther I will come over so we can discuss the idea. Being an incest survivor herself, Esther understands the hell I am going through. She is honest with me about what she has to offer. Esther has her own struggles, yet her heart is vast and roomy. Esther's family have been blessed with hearts as big as hers. Just as Esther predicted, her husband agrees that I should live there. I move in a few days later. It is better than going to a shelter and I am desperate for a place to be. And Esther reminds me of Dr. Davids, who I miss terribly. It is that simple.

Esther and Meir immediately come under attack from my family and the greater Orthodox community. You would think I had been kidnapped against my will. They receive phone calls, letters of criticism, confrontational visits, and threats of retribution in the world to come. Tatty is teaching sixth grade and I am teaching pre-1-A. My director and the principal get involved. I don't know what to think anymore.

I speak to Chavi my boss and pre-school director for a long time. I tell her everything. Chavi validates that some of the teachers in the school, including my father, have messed-up views about sexuality. She says, "I can believe you were emotionally abused, but not physically or sexually. Let's assume it was nothing physical."

I latch on to this denial as if it were a salve. It is a relief for me to believe that the abuse was only emotional and psychological and not physical. I want to believe this is true even more than she does. She validates the younger dissociated part of me, somehow, without really believing her.

Chavi says it is obvious that I was horribly abused and neglected emotionally and psychologically. She validates that I tried to get my parents to see, in every way possible, that I needed help. The more I tried to get them to help me, the more they said that I was crazy, acting strange, and being self-centered.

Her theory is this: In order to survive, my mind had to create something concrete and physical that would make my parents, and others, sit up and say, "Yes, something awful happened."

Then they would validate that I have a right to be angry, and I have a right to hate my parents.

"They messed you up in the worst possible way," Chavi says. "They let you down. The violation was so profound and so destructive that it translated itself into something physical."

Is this plausible or is it just Chavi's denial kicking in?

Would my mind play this kind of trick on me?

Would I have the memories and images of my father molesting me if nothing happened? Are they just another cry for help, as Chavi says?

I'm so confused.

Chavi notices that I have a hard time being angry with my parents. She points out that I always defend them and try to see them as perfect. This is the first time I am able to really hear something like this - without feeling suicidal or crazy. I mean, to listen to her say that maybe I was not physically and sexually abused, that is a relief for me. I wish that she is right and what I remember never actually happened. This makes more logical sense than to think that my father really molested me. I'm not sure where the younger part of me is on this. She feels validated by Chavi no matter which way it actually happened. She feels heard by Chavi, which is something she never experienced from my parents. So we are holding on to this theory right now.

I realize I must distance from my family to unravel the knots and rid myself of the poisonous messages I grew up with. It is so hard to believe that feeling bad is not the same as being bad. It's so hard to accept that as a child I did what I had to do to survive.

Last night I had a body memory. I was in physical pain. I kept startling and crying out and trying to protect my private parts with my hands. From what? What is going on? Why do I disassociate? Doesn't that mean there was a specific trauma? Why do I regress? Why did I feel so sure about this talking to my sister?

Will I ever know the truth?!

Esther gives me a journal inscribed with this poem:

> *Dear Genendy,*
> *I hear the voices also*
> *screams of agony and pain*
> *wait, what is that?*
> *A voice calling*
> *a whisper*
> *urging us on*
> *letting us know*
> *we are not forgotten*
> *Wait... listen...*
> *she is getting louder*
> *Yes, yes I hear her strength,*
> *I feel her surging*
> *getting louder*
> *A power that demands we hear*
> *Oh, the words that have kept us alive*
> *I am a SURVIVOR,*
> *All my love,*
> *Esther*

I miss my family terribly, but there is no turning back.

Displaced

I tell Tanta Rivka about my memories of Tatty molesting me. I have always been close with her.

Tanta Rivka's reaction is not concern, empathy or the offer of support I had hoped for. She has one important question on her mind:

"Can you marry a *kohen* (priest)?" A priest is forbidden by Jewish law from marrying a widow or divorcee. The Torah doesn't really discuss the issue of marrying a victim of incest.

I really don't know the answer to that question and it worries me because I am dating, believe it or not. I am 20 years old. Tatty says if I get married it will solve all of my problems. I call Rabbi Weingart and tell him I have a *shaila* (religious question).

"How can I help you?" He waits expectantly.

"If I was raped by my father can I marry a *kohen*?" Silence. Rabbi Weingart is a friend of my father. Tatty *davened* in his *shul* for many years. Tatty taught his boys in school and helped one of them through some challenges. Rabbi Weingart was my brother's *mohel* (one who performed the ritual) at his *bris* (circumcision). He has been to every family event and knows Zaidy from his years in *yeshiva*. I'm sure he doesn't want to be hearing this question, but I need to know. Finally, I get a response. "Was it before or after age three?" he asks.

"After."

More silence.

Then, "If you say it happened, then no, you cannot marry a *kohen*. But if you say it didn't happen, then yes, you can marry a *kohen*."

That is the end of the conversation. He does not ask me any further questions. Nor does he express any concern at my question. I could have been asking him if my meat fork that I accidentally used in the dairy bowl needed to be koshered. The fact that a young woman with a terribly painful question was crying out to him, reaching out to him for help at the other end of the phone, a real person with feelings, from a family he knows, doesn't register at all in his reaction.

My two worlds are about to collide with a shocking explosion. My inner world of trauma, chaos and shame is about to crash with my outer world of my functional working self. The illusion that my family really loves me, knows what is best for me, and is trying to help me is about to come crashing down. The black wall that always protected me from this con-tradiction is crumbling.

I am still in contact with my family, even though they deny my reality. My married sister who lives in town, Gittel, invites me for *Shabbos* and hol-idays. I go to her, knowing that my pain is not real to her. I have to wrap invisible duct tape around my mouth to keep the screams inside from emerging in a place that is not safe.

Even if I screamed, my sisters would not hear. In their minds, my trauma and my pain do not exist. Therefore, when I am with them, I feel like I do not exist.

Spending time with my family hurts so deeply. I continue a relationship with them out of desperation. They are my family and I love them. I need them. I can't bear them denying my pain, but I cannot live without them either. I don't know what they see when they look at me. I cry myself to sleep every night curled around my pillow in the fetal position. What does God want from me? Why is He doing this to me?

Silence is my only answer. It mocks me. I want to kill myself just to check if there really is a God. It is hard to believe that a kind, loving God would allow a child to suffer as I did.

I am dazed and immobile, as if lying in a pool of blood. My parents and family, all 11 siblings, all of my aunts, uncles, and cousins are determined to keep the shameful secret hidden. They either ignore me or step over my shattered self as I lie here, not quite dead, yet unable to live. I can't ignore the pain and flashbacks. They shrug, indifferent to my pain.

"Get up," is their constant message. "Nothing happened. You're not really hurt. You're making this up. You did this to yourself."

I need my family, but having a relationship right now goes against my need to survive. My family must kill off the part of me that remembers. I must kill it off as well in order to have a relationship with them. The only way to kill off the memories is to kill myself. I am stuck. I have to choose between my survival and my family. I make the choice to live. But I do not know how to continue living in a world without my family. The pain and loneliness are crushing. I beg God to remove me from the world.

I have been in a fog for weeks now, sitting *shiva* in my mind for my parents and siblings. Of course, not one person came to make a *shiva* call because no one really died. I am all alone in my grief. I am a ghost.

At Esther's house, I am finally real. I exist. Being allowed to exist is what every child wants and needs. I do not have to pretend to be okay when I'm not. And I am not okay at all. I want to die. I feel I deserve to die. I betrayed my family and myself by remembering and talking about the unthinkable, unimaginable, and unspeakable. I am accusing my father and my grandfather, a respected *talmid chacham*, of the worst possible thing in the world. I am steeped in shame. And at Esther's house, I can be exactly as I am.

In Esther's basement, I cry for hours when no one is home. I scream into a pillow, using my voice to pound back against the pain and horror of who I am. The flashbacks are unrelenting. They are tearing my mind and soul to shreds.

Tatty, why?!! How?! When?! What did you do to me?! How can I live with this? How can I believe for a second that you did this?? How will I ever survive this? How will I get out alive?

I need to scream and scream. *I'm afraid I will kill you if I ever get in touch with the anger. I'm afraid I really will. You hurt me so badly. You almost destroyed me! Do you really not remember?! Why don't you admit to what you did?! Why don't you take responsibility for your perverted actions?!* I'm terrified.

Voices scream in my head. Terrifying black voices. I think they want me to kill myself. I am very close to the edge. I fear my mind will snap. I so desperately need my family's support and validation. I don't want memories of being sexually abused by my father, grandfather or anyone else. I didn't ask for them. And yet they are here, along with images and feelings of intense shame, rage and terror. I am not supposed to remember these things. I certainly am not supposed to be talking about them. Yet, I can't make them go away. I am destroying myself and my family by knowing, by feeling, by telling. I cannot imagine what God wants from me.

I dream that I am pushing my head hard into the wall to get away. I wake up screaming in the middle of the night banging my head. The physical pain helps distract me from the psychic pain. Meir holds a pillow in front of my head to keep me from hurting myself.

I regress to a two-year-old on the floor of Esther's kitchen. I cry and cry. Esther holds me close. There is no judgment. My feelings are real and allowed. I am real and allowed. Being real, and being allowed to feel, is so new to me. It is overwhelming to finally have permission to feel and talk about what was hidden inside me until now. Esther and Meir are keeping me alive with their love and commitment to me. I know I can trust them in a way I had never been able to trust anyone else before.

I mourn the loss of the family I thought I had. The family I thought loved me and would help me, just because I need their help so badly. Their denial and rejection of my reality makes me realize that the loving family I thought I had was just a fantasy. I was showing signs from a very young age that something was wrong and that I needed help, but no one wanted to know, or to see, that I was being sexually abused. No one had acknowledged my pain and helped me then, and no one will help me now. As a young child, I held on to the fantasy that I was in a safe family in order to survive. Now the fantasy bubble is bursting with an agonizingly painful pop.

My parents' friends are pressuring Esther to kick me out. They seem to be unaware that if I weren't in Esther's home, I would be in a homeless shelter. There is a determination and effort to get me to leave Esther's and move back to my family. How dare Esther and Meir do such a horrible thing, snatching a child from such a wonderful home, stealing her from her wonderful family, and corrupting her!? It is easier to blame and demonize Esther and Meir than to wonder why a young girl would voluntarily flee a supposedly loving, supportive home.

My brother Tzvi warns Esther when he comes to deliver *mishloach manos* (gifts of food) on the holiday of Purim. "Watch your back!" he says to

Esther. Then he turns on me. "How could you think that Tatty and Zaidy abused you? You imagine everyone abused you. Your list keeps getting longer. Who are you going to accuse next, me?"

Tatty approaches Meir at a wedding. "You know you can't believe anything Genendy says," he says.

"I can, and I do," Meir responds. "Your daughter needs help and you're not helping her. I believe what I see."

A neighbor whose daughter is friends with Esther's daughter confronts Esther. "Would you do the same thing to me?" she demands to know. "Would you take my daughter from me, like you took Genendy from her family? How would you feel if the tables were turned, and I took your daughter away from you?!"

Esther is very clear: "God help me, Shaindy, but if my daughter was ever in the situation that Genendy is in now, and you took her in for me, I hope I would have the sense to say thank you."

Esther tells me about a visit from my mother, and I brace myself for the inevitable. I am sure it is all over and I will be asked to leave. Why would Esther and Meir, or anyone else, want to be in the middle of my mess?

"Your mother is very concerned about you being here, but I want to be very clear that we will *not* ask you to leave," she says. "Our home is a safe place for you. We are here for you."

It is hard to believe, but it is true. Esther and Meir do not buckle under pressure from anyone. They reassure me many times that their home is a safe place for me.

And it is. I am emotionally safe for the first time in my life, and the flashbacks are intense. I cry, and shake, and feel unbearable physical pain. I need to hide and there is nowhere to go. I crawl into Leah's linen closet in her bathroom to try to escape the pain and to feel safe. But I can't outrun or hide from the flashbacks.

Dr. Cohen says I am suffering from symptoms of severe post-traumatic stress.

Memories of Tatty molesting me are inside my body and mind, violating me. Intense feelings of being touched and hurt by him invade every sleeping and waking moment. I can't get away from them. The more I try to rationalize, minimize and deny their existence, like he and the rest of my family does, the more they invade my mind and body, insisting I listen and pay close attention.

I am living in terror, and not just because of my memories.

I have done the unthinkable. I left my parents' home against their will. Leaving is a public shaming and betrayal of my *chashuv* (important) family. I know my parents will try anything to get me back home.

Mommy

When I am at my lowest point, Esther tells me, "Sometimes it takes more strength to fall apart and put the pieces back together than never to fall apart in the first place."

Her words make me think of my mother. I once asked my mother if she was sad when her mother died when she was 15.

"A little," she told me.

I asked her then if she remembered being angry as a child. My mother only remembered getting angry once in her life, and she told me about the incident. She had been a child then. I had seen her angry as an adult more than once, and sometimes for good reason! But she didn't call it anger.

"I am upset," she would say.

Why can't I dull my feelings the way my mother is able to? Why can't I erase or stuff my unwanted feelings and memories the way my mother wants me to? "You have no reason to be sad or angry," she often told me.

I try to do what she wanted. I want to be a good girl. I want my mother to love me.

She must be right. She is my mother, after all. I have no reason to feel, no reason to be hurting, no right to exist if my being causes others pain.

Where is mother?
Oh thank goodness,
she's right here next to me.
I reach out to her.
As always, she pushes me firmly away.
You don't want me.
Don't need me.

Where is mother?
I watch her
so painfully close and untouchable.
Only once a day before sleep,
Ma don't forget to kiss me.
Quickly her lips
brush my forehead.
Good night.
Sleep well.

Morning.
I quietly stand by her bed
watching her
peacefully sleep.
Longing aches in my chest.
I love her but
I wish she would
sleep forever,
and only wake up
if I need to tell her something.
Death seems too permanent
too punishing.
Sleep is just fine.
Sleep mother, sleep.
And stop torturing me.

My mother calls and offers to take me on a vacation to a hotel for a few days to talk about our relationship. I feel elated that she cares enough to want to help. But at this point it is too little, too late. The thought of being alone with her revolts and terrifies me.

I know she cannot believe or accept what I desperately need to talk about.

I need to talk to her about my memories of her husband, my father, and her father molesting me. I think about the fact that I never even saw my mother in a bathing suit. I think about how closed and protective she is of her body. She won't even let me see inside her mouth. She often sits with her lips pressed tightly together as if guarding something from entering or escaping. I wonder if she was molested, too.

I need to talk about why I can't stay at home, and why I can't function.

I need to ask her why she didn't protect me when I was little, and why she won't believe me and help me now. I need to talk about my shame and self-hatred. I can't talk to her about any of this, so I stop talking to her altogether.

And I miss her. Because there were things about my mother I could always count on. Good things. This is what is so crazy-making about my mother. My mother has a sense of humor and she is generally kind and patient. She can be playful. She is gentle. She is often respectful. She is deferential. She is opinionated. She cares about people. She asks about my day. She always says goodbye and goodnight. She is not mean, lazy, vindictive or angry. She is definitely "out of the box" in her own way. She does what she believes is right and doesn't care what anyone thinks. She is a thinking, thoughtful person. Not impulsive in the least.

And yet, and yet…

Where *is* she? Where *was* she? My mother let me down so deeply. So completely.

It is like her arms are broken and she doesn't know it. Her broken arms can't hold me. She cannot understand or deal with my feelings, my intensity, my desires, my needs, in a way that holds me and feels safe. She cannot accept me. I frighten her. I have to stay at a distance. There is always something about me she needs to squelch. To reject. Something that is unacceptable to her mind that she can't quite acknowledge. She tells me I have too many feelings.

She taught me that I am too sensitive, too intolerant, too angry. She taught me that I am too needy, too demanding. I am just too hungry - to know, and to learn, and to connect. I am too passionate.

I am simply too much. I want my mother to see me, to know me, to love me and accept me.

Who doesn't want that from their mother? My mother and father are deeply committed to each other. I never heard either of them put the other one down in any way.

When I tell my friends this, they look at me like I'm crazy. My parents never yell at each other or fight like children. Never. Mommy, in Tatty's eyes, can do no wrong. She is his beautiful angel, a gift to him from heaven. He always told me he is the luckiest man alive, that he doesn't deserve her. Mommy always said she hoped that Tatty would die before her, because she would be just fine without him, but he would not be able to go on without her. Mommy doesn't need anyone. Not even me.

What does my mother know?

Mommy keeps Tatty in line. Like me, there are things about my father that need close supervision, things that are dangerous and could get out of control if she would let them. Mommy forbade Tatty to teach girls. She does not let him speak to other women. She keeps Tatty very close and he loves that about her. He listens to her and takes her opinions very seriously. I have the security of knowing that nothing could get in between my parents. Nothing. Certainly not me.

What does my mother know?

My parents need each other a lot more than they need me. Their commitment to each other goes legions beyond their commitment to me. I know that I have to somehow manage on my own. It leaves me out in the cold. I have nowhere to turn but *away* from my parents if I want to survive.

And I so badly want to survive.

I pull your faces toward me out of the past
My mother
My father
I touch your faces
I look into your eyes
I pinch your faces hard
Trying to make you see me
Feel me
I want you to feel my pain and anger

I yell in your blank faces,
"Why didn't you help me?!
Don't you even see me?
Have you ever once seen me?
I needed help!"

Your puzzled eyes gaze calmly at each other
Are you amused by my intense feelings, Mommy?
Is the half smile on your lips your way of blocking my feelings?
Is that how you keep me away?
My feelings are not real and so you are safe from them?

Your lips move,
"Do you know what she's talking about Tatty?"
"No Mommy, we'd better go discuss it."

You turn together, the two of you, and walk in step to your bedroom
to discuss what to do about me
You are on an important mission
A mission that excludes me
You will close the door and decide together what you will do
By the time you come out
...I'll be gone
Then you will go back to your room to discuss my leaving
Together
Forever
In step

One day, after living with Esther and Meir for about half a year, I get a letter in the mail. It is from my mother.

My Dear Beloved Genendy,

It hurts me very much that I'm not expressing myself to you verbally the way I would like to. So I'm resorting to pen and paper.

It's important to me that you know I feel you are very solid in your personality, in your goodness, and in your yiddishkeit, your religiosity. That's always what I console myself with when I worry about you.

You might say, in that case why worry? Well I am a mother, your mother, and I really feel a responsibility toward you. It's not in me to missionize the world (even though I have an opinion on everything), only those closest to me where I honestly feel it's my place to do so.

The way I understand it, it seems that there are many things to be angry about and to complain about, that makes it difficult to function. But when it comes down to a crisis you are in full control and manage to do whatever has to be done. Even though I know you try extremely hard, I'm asking, "Is it possible for a person to always be in full control?"

I also feel, when you disagree with me, instead of just disagreeing you become angry at my whole being, which I feel is really unfair.

Whether I agree with you or not I feel it's a courtesy to hear me out and allow my input even if you politely discard it.

I hope you feel my well-meaning feelings which are so difficult for me to convey.

Wishing you always the best.

With loving feelings,
Ma

Dear Genendy,

Thanks for writing again. I appreciate so much hearing from you. I've wracked my brain and thought long and hard, how we were as a family, how Tatty interacted with you and all the children, how my father was, how it's pretty difficult to pull one over me. I've come to the conclusion that there was no abuse. I feel I am always honest with myself and don't have any "subconscious defenses." Sometimes I have a thought which I don't feel is proper to share with anyone but Ta. With Tatty and myself I'm always completely open and honest.

In what way do you feel I'm not "respecting your boundaries?" Are you asking me to respect your imagination? (That is what it is to me.) Does a person need their thoughts and imagination validated? We both mentioned and agree that disagreement does not mean disrespect. I really have no ulterior motives in not answering or telling you my feelings about "the abuse" which I truly believe just never was.

Always happy to hear from you.

Lots of love and a kiss,
Ma

Dear Genendy,

I miss you too. Could we make up to meet somewhere?

How do you think someone deals with feelings? By talking about them? I didn't mean you should not talk about your pain for your healing. Of course, that's not Lashon Hara [gossip]. I was referring to that you said Zaidy abused other people!

Do you really believe a person is not supposed to give of themselves unto others? In a physical sense, when we give of our money and time we of course don't have it for ourselves. In a spiritual sense, I think sometimes it's the same.

My memories of you as a child: You did speak to us and tell us your feelings and how you felt about things. Are my memories all wrong?

Obviously, I was and am missing a recognition of your sensitivities and pain for which I hope you forgive me. I wasn't there in the way you needed.

As I try, I want to improve. Hopefully I will. Thank you for your input which can only help things along.

Waiting to hear from you.

Lots of love and more,
Ma

Dear Ma,

How do YOU think someone deals with feelings? Who is "someone?" I deal with my feelings in many different ways. My pain, that you agree that I should talk about in order to heal, is that Zaidy and Tatty and other people molested me. What did you think my pain is?! My grandfather who was supposedly a talmid chacham did this to me. My family who is supposedly a frum family. My father, a rebbe, molested me when I was just a baby. I'm crying as I write this. How could he do this to me? I needed him. Why did he hurt me like that? You yourself told me that Zaidy abused you physically. So did some of your siblings. (Don't act so outraged that I would say such a thing.) It is a lot safer for a child to believe that the world is really safe. That the people who were supposed to protect me were good. It was easier for me to believe there must be something bad or disgusting about ME that made them have to hurt me. <u>I won't believe this anymore</u>. I won't kill myself because of what Tatty did. I don't need to punish myself for their bad actions. This is a family sickness that started before I came along. I did nothing to cause it. In order to heal I need to put the responsibility back where it belongs. On the abusers. On Zaidy and Tatty, and other perverts in that sick yeshiva.

A person cannot give what he doesn't have. You cannot give of yourself unless you actually have a self to give. That's why children are naturally more "selfish." They are in the process of developing a self. Once a healthy self is established, the person giving, although benefiting others, is ultimately giving to himself. Lighting another flame does not diminish from the original one. I strongly disagree with you on this. Genuine giving is NOT self-destructive. It is quite the opposite. Giving up a part of yourself is suicide. I always felt like you were trying to take myself away from me. Trying to kill me. That's why I never wanted you near me. Of course, as a child I talked to you about my feelings. That's why I'm so angry with you! You're not stupid. Don't pretend you didn't know I was troubled. You taught me that even though I was sad and angry my job was to put a smile on my face. Just stuff your feelings so everything will be fine, right? Wrong! I hate what you did to me. You practically destroyed me. And now you play the Memory Game, picking out the memories that "match" your fantasy.

Well, I'm not so good at that game. I remember the bad things too. Your denial sickens me. It's very small comfort that you can admit that you're obviously missing something. I wonder why you choose to ignore my questions and references to the abuse. I believe that a part of you really knows the truth. But the ramifications are too much for you to handle. Intellectually I know that I live because God wants me to. I don't need your permission to exist. I get the feeling that you and the family are hoping that one day I'll wake up and realize that I'm making a mistake. That I need my family and I'll come back home and live happily ever after. This is as unrealistic as thinking that one day our brain-damaged cousin will wake up and act and speak like a normal five-year-old. It's hard to accept that both scenarios just aren't going to happen. Thank God I have many good friends who appreciate me and accept me for who I am and not who they want me to be. I don't need you to tell me who I am. I don't need you to tell me that I was abused. I know already that both of those are truths. Although it is painful I can exist without you and without the family. Please don't think that I know you well enough to assume anything about you. I don't feel as if I know you very well.

I know people who knew the girl personally, from the Readers' Digest article that you sent me about False Memory Syndrome. They said that it was obvious to anyone who knew her that her parents were up to their eyeballs in cults. They put so much pressure on her to recant her memories that she finally sold out on herself.

No one can make up that kind of abuse.

Every child wants to have normal loving parents.

We would all rather believe that we imagined everything.

Sincerely,
Genendy

Dear Genendy,

Your letter was loaded, I appreciate so much your writing. Whenever you're ready I would like to meet with you and discuss these issues a little bit at a time. In the meanwhile, it's not that I'm avoiding the issues, it's just I feel we're in such disagreement about so many facts. I don't want to just refute you. I'd like to discuss with you. We're sort of arguing whether the "chair is blue or pink." We each have rights.

Do people have to be in agreement to live with and respect each other? I know I'm not the kind of person who is at all for show, knowing myself I would never ignore a wrong done by one member of the family to cover up for another.

I know you were troubled. Many times, I tried to help you in my way. Obviously, you needed a different way of help. A way that does not come naturally to me, but which I would "dig" into myself for. I hope you'll forgive me for not helping you the way you needed.

Waiting to hear from you.

Lots of love and a kiss,
Ma

Dear Ma,

I wrote you this already, and I will write once again: <u>It is disrespect-ful to call the abuse that I suffered my imagination.</u> There is NO WAY you can possibly know what happened to me <u>if you were not there</u>. If you were to tell me that you had a miscarriage yesterday all I can say is, "I'm sorry." I would not be so insensitive and dishonest as to say that I'm sure it was your imagination! How can I know?

Can you see that it's possible that you cannot be honest with your-self about my memories of Tatty? You would have to re-evaluate your entire life and marriage, beliefs and values. In short, all the supposed "facts of your life" would suddenly be up in the air. (I dare Tatty to swear in the name of God that he never molested me!)

There are many kinds of boundaries. Your reality versus mine is only one example. When one respects you for who you are it means he respects your thoughts, feelings and reality. This is obviously differ-ent from seeing me as I see myself. I feel like we've gone through this three times. I think you're in denial about the possibility that I might be telling the truth, and there is no way you can know. You really seem to believe these things. A part of me feels bad for you because I know that I will be okay. I am learning to love and care for myself. I am learning to be clear about who I am and what I need. I am healing. I wonder if you'll ever have the courage to do that. It takes a lot of strength. A lot of tears. I'm sorry you're hurting. I wish you could write an honest letter to yourself about how you feel about me. Pretend you won't send it to me. Don't send it to me. Just try to be real. That's what I want from you. That's what I need from you. This is what I've always needed. For you to be honest with yourself and with me.

With all due respect.

Your daughter,
Genendy

Dear Ma,

I'm writing to tell you that I won't be writing again for a while. I just don't have the energy right now to deal with your denial. I think I made it clear to you what my needs are. I think you made it clear that you cannot fill those needs. When I said that I need you to respect my boundaries and my reality, I meant that even though, to you, the abuse is my imagination, to me the abuse was, and still is, very real. I am asking you to respect that by NOT CALLING IT MY IMAGINATION!! You don't seem to understand the meaning of respect for boundaries. There is no way you can possibly know if I was abused or not unless you were with me every second (which you obviously weren't). I know you tend to see things in black and white, so it would be hard for you to realize that you don't need to validate the abuse for me, OR disrespect my reality by saying it never happened. Another option is to admit that you don't know, which you really don't.

Anyone can abuse a child. All a person needs to have is the ability to turn off their feelings. If they would think for a minute how the child is feeling they would not be able to hurt them. I have seen and experienced Tatty doing this countless times. I know and am human enough to admit that I do have subconscious defenses. I do not always have the ability to be completely open and honest with myself. This is a process that for me takes constant work and awareness. It's interesting that you see yourself as being so perfect in this difficult area. I believe that it is our yetzer hara [evil inclination] or subconscious and conscious defenses against the truth that allow us to sin. Maybe you were born without a yetzer hara? How do you know that you are always completely open and honest? Are you God? I know that the trauma that I experienced affected every aspect of myself. I am a product of the abuse. Calling it my imagination is implying that I am a product of imagination and don't really exist.

This is nothing new. I never felt like I existed to you. As a child I needed you to validate my existence as every child does. I finally learned that in order for me to exist I would have to leave the family. The choice is to live with the pain that to my family I don't exist, or to die with it. I hope I will not kill myself because of you. I find myself considering the option pretty frequently. You don't want to believe that Tatty did those things? I don't either. Who would? You think I'm enjoying this? You think I like not having parents, not having a family? You think I enjoy being in mental hospitals? The dissociative disorder that I have is a result of severe and repeated trauma that began in early childhood. I'm not crazy. Why would I make this up? There must be other reasons you can't believe this. Tell me honestly, why won't you believe me? Try to be honest. It's the least you can do. And maybe try to answer my questions from the other letters. We cannot meet until you can tell me the following:

1. That I have a right to my feelings and my memories, even though yours are different.

2. That I can trust myself.

3. That I have a right to be angry with you for hurting me so badly.

4. That I can do what I need to do to heal. I can honestly validate all of the above for you. You are certainly entitled to your memories, feelings and healing. I can only tell you how I see things, my experiences of you, and my memories.

Sincerely,
Genendy

My Dear, Dear Genendy,

Thank you so much for writing again. Genendy, the tone in your letter sounds so impatient with me, please excuse me for being so slow to get the gist of it, but I really do want to understand your needs. I hope in the near future you will be able to find the energy for me. Whenever you do I'll be happy to hear from you again. Even though you don't need me, I <u>do</u> need you, and a relationship with you. I will wait and hope for the best.

Please forgive me if it sounds repetitious, maybe it's because as you say, to me everything has to be "black and white," but I truly am trying to understand you, and to get things clearer to me.

I do realize that to you the abuse is real and part of you. Am I called disrespectful to you because it's not part of me?

When you say "boundaries" do you mean your reality versus my reality?

When someone respects you for who you are, does that mean they perceive you as you see yourself?

When you tell me I'm in denial, what am I denying? I'm not denying that you feel abused.

On that subject of honesty, isn't honesty something only a person themselves can know? Are you telling me that a person can't even tell on themselves if they are honest or not?

I don't know why it seems to take me so long to get things clear.

All my love and more,
Ma

Anger

Black waves of rage engulf me in a flood of intense fury
Crushing me

Drowning me
I scream, a silent cry of despair

A tense helpless agony burns inside
I know I cannot escape it
Instinctively, I dive head first into the raging violence
Shouting and screaming against the terrible pressure
I pound and kick and fight my way down, down, down
Through the terrifying anger to the feelings beneath
I lie exhausted, still at the bottom
My face is wet and
I am shaking, and feeling
The sadness, fear, guilt and shame I had buried deep under a turbu-
lent sea of anger
I finally found the courage to face.

Esther gives me what I never had and always needed: unconditional acceptance. She reassures me that it is okay to get the help I need. I deserve to be safe. She believes I deserve to survive.

But at a certain point, Esther realizes that I need more. Esther takes me to the hospital when I become too suicidal to stay safe in her home.

In the months of exchanging letters with my mother, I am hospitalized three times. I can't seem to figure out the truth of who I am and what really happened. My family is not helpful in this.

After a while I decide to leave Esther's. I am so unstable that it feels unfair to her and her family for me to stay longer. I live with a friend of hers, another survivor with ten children, for a few weeks before I am asked to leave because my presence made her teenage son uncomfortable. Once again, I have nowhere to go.

I leave my job in the school where Tatty works. I just can't face my sisters and father every day. I then apply for a job in another pre-school opening up in the neighborhood, and I am hired. I am then promptly fired when community members pressure the school not to let me work there.

Since I moved out of my parents' house, the community assumes there is obviously something wrong with me.

My new boss consults with, of all people, my first therapist, Dr. Davids, who advises her not to let me teach. Now I have another reason to resent Dr. Davids. I was depending on this job to pay for rent, therapy, food, etc.

I am desperate. I am isolated, unemployed and homeless.

I desperately need to get on disability. I apply, I am rejected and I apply again. This time I am approved. Thank God, I have money for rent and food.

I move to my own basement apartment. I also do a bit of babysitting. The family I am babysitting for gives me an old T.V. It keeps me company at night.

I get a present from Tatty, a book by Miriam Adahan called *Nobody's Perfect*. Tatty knows that I spoke with Miriam and I like her. She is the only one who I told who believes me and doesn't think I'm crazy. Tatty marked some of the pages with scotch tape. I've already gone through them a few times to try to understand what Tatty is trying to tell me. On page 113 at the bottom paragraph Tatty underlined some words. *People have* <u>*problems*</u> *which either* <u>*need to be solved*</u> *or* <u>*ignored*</u>. *We cannot do either if we are whipping ourselves into an emotional frenzy.*

The underlined words read "<u>problems need to be ignored</u>." He thinks I am making a big deal out of nothing. He's probably right. And it can't possibly be solved anyway. On page 160 Tatty drew a circle around these words: *Don't focus on other people's faults. It's no sign of great genius to see what's wrong with others. Anyone can do that. The real gift is to see the good and to reinforce it both in yourself and others.* Tatty doesn't want me to blame him or hold him responsible for what he did to me when I was a little girl. He wants me to focus on the love and care that he also gave me and still wants to offer me. Why can't I just focus on the good??

On page 240 Tatty underlined this: <u>*Don't approach others from a position of need. Instead, be to others what you want others to be to you*</u>. *Your neediness drives people away. It bores, suffocates and frightens people. Even the most patient person cannot be always available, understanding and sympathetic. Instead you be empathic and understanding. You be the caring friend you want others to be. Give to others!*

Tatty wants me to take care of myself, and of him too. I am not allowed to have needs or to need help. I know I am breaking the rules by asking for help. On page 242 he underlined: <u>*forgiveness toward those who hurt you.*</u>

I'm glad he knows that he hurt me. But how can I forgive him if he won't help me stay alive?!

The next chapter is called *Don't think like a terrorist*, and Tatty underlined: <u>*Say three words of*</u> *appreciation* <u>*to my family members*</u>. And in the last sentence, Tatty underlined his final message to me: *The* <u>*gift of light becomes our own*</u> *when we succeed in* <u>*overcoming the darkness of hatred*</u>.

I don't hate you Tatty!

I hate what you did to me.

I hate what you are still doing to me.

Tatty, help me.

I am dying.

PART 5:

FALLING

Memories

I see myself in a broken glass mirror of shattered memories.
My reflection is cloudy
the image distorted by cracks,
splinters, missing pieces.
How was my mirror broken?
By whom?
Are parts still missing?
I am very close,
but afraid to wipe the cloud of steam from the surface
and see the true picture
behind it.
So I take apart the fragments to study each one separately,
and my identity splits, and is lost,
along with my reflection.

This is the last straw. My second therapist, Dr. Cohen, stops seeing me because I found out personal information about her. It was my fault, too. I got a job working for a kosher diet program and she had been a client there. Some intake forms were put in front of me and I was told to file them. Hers was among them. I read a few lines before I filed the pages. I felt so guilty. I had violated my therapist's privacy. And I was stupid enough to tell her about it.

Dr. Cohen is the kind of therapist who never tells me anything about herself. So she calls my boss and screams at her, which promptly gets me fired. She then claims the therapeutic boundaries had been irreparably breached and she can't treat me anymore. She agrees to stay with me until I find a new therapist. When it doesn't go as quickly as she thinks it should, Dr. Cohen terminates treatment, leaving me with no one. Now I don't have a therapist or a job.

120

If my family really believe I am crazy, why are they so scared of me that they won't help me? They helped Tanta Leah when she was crazy. Why do they want me to die? Why did they run out of my life and leave me so alone, and in pain?

Spiritual Death

So this is what it's like to die a spiritual death
the body is here
but the soul is gone
leaving a rotten core of nothingness
and desolate feelings
spinning slowly in lonely isolation
around and around making
useless aimless circles
of sadness.
Spiraling down a deep vacuum
knowing that the self has split into pieces
and disintegrated
leaving this empty useless body
with its core of rot
and its heart ripped to shreds.

Perhaps I am sane and speaking the truth and they can't deal with that. I cannot imagine what God wants from me. Better I should die than cause a *chillul Hashem* (disgracing the name of God). Better I should die than live with a family who cannot accept my existence. I want to die, if only to find out the truth.

Suicide

I have been living alone, isolated in a basement, for a few months now. Friends of mine find me a job taking care of four young children every day from 4PM to 8PM. I serve them dinner, help them with homework and get them ready for bed. It is my only connection to sanity. They call me "Mary Poppins" and we have a lot of fun together. I must seem normal otherwise why would these parents allow me to care for their children?

I take a risk and share what I am going through with the children's parents. The father approaches me nervously a few days later. He read somewhere that adults who were molested could molest other children. The children's father makes me swear I would never hurt his kids. In shock and horror, I swear.

I know I love these children and would never hurt them.

But now I feel like a perpetrator.

I remember when I felt this way before. I was essentially homeless, living between Esther's house and a mental hospital, staying with friends, Lisa and David, for a few months. I was lying on a mattress in Lisa's spare room reading the book *Thou Shalt Not Be Aware* by Alice Miller. The book is validating on so many levels. At the same time, I couldn't help wishing I was less aware, or even better, completely unaware of child abuse at all.

Two years ago, when I was 19, the two of them had tried to set me up with a very nice 27-year-old friend of theirs. I actually liked the guy, and he told Lisa I was the first person who he ever dated who was serious about Torah learning. I dated him three times before he broke it off. He told Lisa that he sensed that I was anxious being near him. He was right. On our second date, he took me rowing, and when he took off his socks and shoes to get into the wet boat, I looked away in discomfort. No one in my family would ever take their socks off in front of a stranger. In fact, I remember my mother telling me that for the first few nights after marrying Tatty, she didn't take her stockings off before bed at all. Was this man's behavior normal? I was very aware of my lack of a helpful barometer for normal. I found myself keeping a careful distance walking beside him on the third date, suddenly aware that I had issues with men. I guess he was aware as well, because he broke off with me.

This one night, I found myself drifting off to sleep to the sound of Lisa's two adorable little girls, three-year-old Yael and two-year-old Sara, playing before bed. Suddenly, I was startled to feel someone move my blanket and climb into bed beside me. It was Lisa's blue-eyed blond curly haired two-year-old daughter, Sara. I froze. *What was Sara doing, climbing into my bed?* It must be very early morning. Sara barely knew me, but she obviously liked and trusted me, but why?

She shouldn't trust me. Trusting me is so wrong. What if I am a child molester like Tatty? What if I reached down and touched her? I could do it in a second and she, being asleep, and so young, would never know what happened, and would be forever broken, like I was. Maybe I would be doing her a favor to abuse her, and teach her not to trust so easily. Aren't all little girls eventually molested? Am I nuts?! Of course I wouldn't touch her! But how can I be sure? After all, children trust Tatty, he is good with them, and he molested me and doesn't remember... Maybe I'm just like him!

Oblivious to my terror, Sara snuggled up beside me and went back to sleep. I did not move or breathe deeply, so scared I was of the power inherent in being an adult, alone with a trusting child. I must have fallen asleep, because when I awoke light was streaming through the window, and Sara was gone. I could breathe again.

Now, listening to my employer express his fears, I wonder why would he let me continue to care for his children if he has any doubts that I am safe with them? I am relieved that the job ends soon. I don't trust myself.

My sister Chaya calls me to ask permission to get engaged. Chaya is two years younger than me, and things like marriage go according to age in our family. Oldest siblings get married first. Chaya tells me that she knows I'm not in any position to think about marriage. She calls out of respect, wanting to ask my permission before becoming engaged ahead of me, her older sister.

I tell her it is fine with me. I am in no condition to think about marriage.

I have no support, no job, no therapist, I am struggling with severe depression and post-traumatic stress symptoms, and I am suicidal. I tell Chaya I am seriously depressed. I tell her I am thinking of killing myself. I tell her I can't handle the fact that no one believes me. I must have said it more than once before.

Chaya says, "Why don't you stop talking about it and just do it already?"

When Chaya speaks these words, verbalizing what I already sense is the family's death wish for me, I start piling up pills.

I have a whole bunch of prescriptions for depression and anxiety that hadn't worked for me. I write a suicide note in a brand-new journal with two cuddly kittens on the front.

Jan 3, 1995

I would like to free my tortured soul from this body. We hate the body and what it says and does. We can't be normal. No one believes. No one helps. I don't know what will happen tonight. The fight inside is intense. Trying to keep my distance leaves me feeling numb and unreal. I don't really care if I live or die. I want to go to God and see truth. I've been too long in this world of lies.

One thing I want to leave behind me if I die is this: My father sexually abused me. I have no doubts. He may not remember, just as I didn't for a while, but he did do it. I am the result of his abuse. My father has been, in a way, so helpful, and so hurtful. So have my therapists. So, it seems, is God. He gives and takes away, helps and hurts, creates and destroys.

Speak up about sexual abuse in the frum community. It is there among your leaders. Speaking up is the only way to stop it. I know the feeling of wanting to abuse children. I would rather kill myself than come to that. The only difference between me and my father is that I tried to take responsibility for what was done to me. He never did.

If I go to hell, I'll meet you there Tatty,

Genendy

I fill a cup with water and quickly gulp down handfuls of pills. I take everything I have.

I give it a good shot, loyal daughter and sister that I am. I am hoping to lose consciousness quickly, but it isn't happening fast enough. I am terrified to be alone while I die. I call a crisis hotline that I had been speaking with almost daily. I reassure them that I am just lonely and scared, and have no plans to act on my suicidal thoughts, which they knew about from previous conversations. We speak for a while. I tell them I am getting tired and plan to go to sleep and promise to call them in the morning.

I am unaware that I had started slurring my words. The hotline calls my psychiatrist who prescribed my medication, who calls the upstairs neighbor whose basement I am renting, to check up on me. By the time I am found, I am unconscious. The ambulance takes me to the hospital. My stomach is pumped with charcoal. When I wake up the next day in the ICU, they tell me I am lucky to be alive. A nurse tells me angrily that I had swallowed enough drugs to kill a horse.

I don't feel lucky. I feel like a criminal. I am terrified, ashamed, and angry to be alive.

Even worse, my mother, my brother Tzvi and my sister Chaya show up at the hospital. Somehow they found out about my botched suicide attempt. I will later learn that my psychiatrist called them, not knowing if I would survive. Now I can't trust him either. They are the last people in the world I want to see.

Why won't God just let me die?

State Hospital

> *Angels of madness prowl the hallway*
> *and sneak past the med window into the day hall*
> *where a bent man paces, trying to escape*
> *the darkness in his mind.*
> *A woman, eyes staring and empty,*
> *rocks to the rhythm of her thoughts.*
> *I wonder when her soul left.*
> *A white-haired atttorney carries on intense conversations*
> *with himself.*
> *Desperate shrieks and howls emanate from the quiet room.*
> *I try to get lost in a game of spades.*
> *Unwanted images invade my thoughts.*

Days locked in solitary confinement.
Nights strapped to a bed in six-point restraint.
Today my friend hit a nurse and was taken
away in handcuffs.
I wonder if I'll be next.
Horror and shame this person who is me.
No, don't think!
Focus on the rare moments of light –
moments when wasted addicts hold each other up
on weak arms,
sharing the anguish of daily survival.
Moments of staff kindness –
a hug, a pat, a reassuring word.
Today I'm on level three.
I will be let outside for two precious hours.
Maybe I'll sneak off grounds,
let my tired mind free of the locked doors and locked spirits
of the hospital.
I'll run through the grassy fields,
wade in the creek,
gaze up at the blue sky and shout "Hellooo!!" to God.

I have not seen God behind these walls.

Ms. Green's gray hair frames her chocolate-colored skin. She deals with the boredom of the inpatient psychiatric ward by making it her personal mission to save my troubled soul.

She learns that I am Jewish and she follows me around the day hall with a cup of coffee, deliberately splashing the coffee in my direction.

"I don't want you goin' to hell, so I'm gonna baptize you. Then you be goin' straight to heaven with Jesus."

She doesn't give up until she manages to splash a few drops of coffee on my head.

Now when we pass each other in the day hall she chortles with glee, "You be baptized girl. You goin' straight to heaven!"

Rising to heaven on a few drops of coffee.

I wish it were really that simple.

Waterfall used to be a farming hospital. It is a large campus of rolling green hills and old abandoned buildings. Patients live in newer, more modern buildings. One of the older buildings houses a museum and a clothing boutique for the patients. Another one houses a library and eye clinic. Most of the old buildings are empty, and more commonly used by patients to meet secretly with the opposite sex and break the rules. I find out pretty quickly that here in Waterfall, women commonly sell themselves for a box of "smokes" or cigarettes.

I turn down proposals almost daily.

I start wearing pants and it's not because I am rebelling religiously. Not yet, anyway. It is simply a matter of personal safety.

A number of the patients at Waterfall served time in prison for various, sometimes violent, offenses. The hospital has a level system for behavior management. I make it to Level Three, and I am allowed off the locked ward to walk freely around the large hospital grounds for a few hours a day.

One day I am outside with some fellow patients wearing my Bais Yaakov-style skirt. A male patient, who I am aware has a history of violence, approaches me.

"If I catch you walking alone outside I'm gonna rape you," he warns in a low voice as he walks past.

I march straight back to the ward and report him. I am relieved when he loses his level immediately and is confined to the ward. But the encounter leaves me with the realization that wearing a skirt in Waterfall is not safe or modest.

In fact, my fellow patients confirm that my skirts are attracting dangerous attention to myself. I never see another female patient wearing a skirt, and the men look me up and down as I walk by. I visit the boutique and pick out some jeans and shorts. I feel safer in them. I blend in. I feel a lot more modest.

The incident with the skirt triggers a memory of similar feelings I had when I was three years old. My mother told me that I was "a big girl," and that pants were no longer appropriate for me. I was very upset. I felt safer in pants than skirts. I remember trying to hide a pair of pants in my dresser, but my mother found them and confiscated them. I felt exposed and vulnerable in a skirt. I felt like an easy target for abuse in a skirt, just like I felt at Waterfall.

I make some interesting friends - well, if you can call them that - with two men on my ward, both about 20 years older than me. Gabe is a runner. Adam is Jewish. Both are recovering heroin addicts. The hospital is giving them Methadone, and slowly weaning them off it so they won't die from withdrawal. I am learning all kinds of things I never would have known if I wasn't in the hospital. For example, withdrawal from heroin can be brutal. Adam tells me that he ended up in the hospital because he accidentally injected bleach into his arm instead of heroin. I ask him why he had bleach in the needle in the first place. He said he used the bleach to sterilize the needle.

"Why would you bother sterilizing a needle that you are using to kill yourself with?"

Adam smiles wryly and nods in agreement. "That's drug addiction for you. Completely irrational."

One of the reasons I feel comfortable with Gabe and Adam is because they clearly have no romantic interest in me. They just want to be friends. Maybe they are gay. I don't know.

Adam tells me that he thinks of me as a little sister. We sneak off hospital grounds together and go to the local 7/11, the mall, and the movies, or just for a run.

I can barely keep up with either man, and neither Adam nor I can keep up with Gabe. Today we are running and I tell Gabe and Adam I wish I had some Benadryl. Benadryl is a good way to knock myself out and escape the pain for a while.

We stop at 7/11 and I wait outside for Gabe and Adam, who decide to go in and buy a drink. When they return Adam hands me a pack of Benadryl.

"Thanks," I say, "I'll pay you back."

"Nah, I got it for free."

It takes me a moment to comprehend.

Then my eyes widen. "You stole it!?" I accuse.

"It was easy," Adam shrugs. "Gabe distracted the cashier and I slipped it into my pocket. I did it for you… You wanted Benadryl, didn't you?"

I shove it back into his hands like it bit my finger. "Put it back, right now! Put it back!!"

Adam pats my shoulder like I am having a nervous breakdown. Gabe is looking around nervously. "Here, give it to me," he says, "I'll put it back."

He takes the Benadryl and disappears back into the store. A minute later he reappears and holds up his empty hands for me to see. "I put it back. No worries." He sees me glance at his pockets and turns them inside out for me to inspect. "I put it on the shelf in the back of the store. No one saw me. Relax."

My relationship with Adam and Gabe is teaching me a lot. I am talking to men. Relating to them as real people. Something not done in my family. I am trusting them enough to go on outings alone with them. I am trusting myself that they are not the kind of men who want to hurt me. I am setting boundaries. I am learning to trust my own intuition about people.

I am labeled a lesbian for my lack of interest and involvement in sexual activities, which has its own problems. While the men leave me alone I still have to ward off advances from women.

I receive a birthday card from all of the residents of my ward on my 23rd birthday. It says on the cover, "Happy Birthday to someone who always practices safe sex." Inside is inscribed, "Not having any is pretty darn safe!"

Losing my religion

Not long after my wardrobe adjustment, my oldest sister, Gittel, invites me to the *yeshiva* campus where she lives with her husband and five little girls, for a *Shabbos*. My brother-in-law picks me up at the hospital. I leave in shorts, but carry a skirt in a bag, explaining to him that I plan to change as soon as I arrive at my sister's house.

What am I thinking going to a yeshiva campus in shorts?

Part of the answer is that I'm not convinced that anyone will notice or care.

I feel invisible.

It doesn't seem to register with Gittel and Chaya, my uncle and aunt, (my father's brother Nachi also lives on the *yeshiva* campus) or anyone else in my family, that I am in a crisis, living in a mental hospital, and desperately needing help and support. No one discusses it with me openly, or asks me how I am coping in this dangerous environment. My family says I can leave the hospital and live a normal life anytime I want to. After all, my suffering is my own fault because I caused it.

My trauma and pain are not real, so maybe I'm not real either. Maybe my life is just a bad dream. In a dream you can do whatever you want and it doesn't matter. You can even be a religious, Orthodox girl and wear shorts to a yeshiva.

I borrow a slip from my cousin for *Shabbos*. Sunday morning, I stop by Uncle Nachi's house on the way back to the hospital to return it. When my uncle sees me in his house in shorts he becomes incensed. He sees this as the ultimate in disrespect, a slap in the face.

I see it as a desperate cry for help.

As usual, the wind grabs my cries of pain and whips them back into my face. No one notices or feels my suffering other than me.

My uncle takes one look at me and begins to scream, "Get out of my house!"

He literally picks me up (I am very thin, not more than 100 pounds, but the lack of adequate kosher food in the hospital is another story) and throws me out the front door. I fall on the sidewalk scraping my arms.

I am used to emotional and psychological rejection from my family. His physical rejection is further proof of the emotional rejection I am experiencing daily.

My uncle does not see me, a person, his own niece, in pain. All he sees is a pair of offending shorts and an embarrassment to the family. He violates the laws of *negiya*, forbidden touching of a woman, to throw me out of his house.

Bruised, humiliated, and shocked, I wander away and make my way to the *rosh yeshiva's* house.

Along the way I begin to feel a rage toward Torah that threatens to overwhelm me. My family and the *yeshiva* represent Torah. If the Torah is as shallow as a pair of shorts, it is all a crock, all about appearances, and I want nothing more to do with it anymore.

If I looked "off the *derech*" (off the path, or the way of God) in my shorts before the incident with my uncle, I really am off the *derech* now. I know that God is not shallow.

The *rosh yeshiva* says he will speak with my uncle Nachi.

I speak to the *rebbetzin* (rabbi's wife) for a while. I ask her about her son, Dr. Davids' brother, who is also accused of sexually abusing his students. I ask her if she believes it.

"I have to honestly say," she replies, "that although I hope the allegations against my son are not true, I don't really know. I wasn't there and didn't see what happened."

"I wish my mother and siblings would admit the same thing!" I cry, hit by a pang of jealousy. "How can they insist that they know my father did nothing to me if they didn't see it?"

The *rebbetzin* does not have an answer for me.

I tell the *rosh yeshiva* and his wife, the *rebbetzin*, what my father did to me as a young child. I tell them I am living in a hospital as a result. I ask him to speak to my father.

"Please ask my father to take some responsibility for what he did. I want to have a relationship with him. Someday I want to get married and my father will want to walk me down to the *chuppah* (wedding canopy). I can't stand the thought of him touching me now. I can't continue pretending that nothing happened."

The *rosh yeshiva* promises me that he will speak with my father as well.

I pass through their house like a ghost and will never hear from them again.

A few years later, when I will become engaged to be married, my uncle Nachi will approach me to ask forgiveness for throwing me out his front door. The memory of the agony of that day will well up inside me. I will tell him that his actions were what pushed me to become non-religious. I will tell him that I stopped keeping *Shabbos* and kosher after the incident. But I will also tell him that I forgive him.

But what I will not tell him is that what he didn't do at the time hurt a lot worse than what he did do to me. He never tried to help me, and for that he will never ask forgiveness or be forgiven. He ignored my pain and failed to reach out to me during the most vulnerable period of my life. He blamed me for my suffering and added to my trauma just like the rest of my family did. Ignoring my pain and abandoning me to the streets of a psychiatric hospital are worse than any physical assault.

I am not getting enough food. Fruit and cereal for breakfast. A kosher plane meal for dinner. My mother brings me a box of granola bars. I can buy some snacks from the machine on the ward to fill in some of the missing calories. But I am still losing weight. And I'm always hungry.

A woman patient advocate calls and asks if I need help with anything. I tell her about the food problem and she helps me file a lawsuit against the hospital.

I am invited to a hearing in the hospital grounds. About a dozen people sit around a table in a conference room and eye me. "Look at her," one of the men says as if I am not there. "She is too thin. She needs more food."

I win the case within five minutes. I will get more kosher food.

My advocate congratulates me. Apparently, because of me the law is forever changed. Any Jewish patient in any U.S. state hospital is entitled to three kosher meals a day from now on.

Ironically, soon after I win the case, I stop keeping kosher.

It dawns on me after a year of living in this institution that some people never leave. One man, Sammy, just celebrated his 100th birthday. Sammy is schizophrenic and has been in the hospital since the age of 30. By the time medications became available to allow him to live a normal life he was 60 years old and could not function outside of the hospital. I watch Sammy's bent figure walking slowly around the hospital grounds collecting cans for recycling. I find myself thinking, *That could be me in 80 years.*

I realize the nurses are right – I had better get out of the hospital before I become institutionalized.

I think I am the only one in the drug rehab group who is not a recovering drug addict or alcoholic. I joined the group because I was told that this particular group was the key to leaving the hospital. Dr. D. helps patients transfer to a Christian halfway house, the Elizabeth House, in a seedy section downtown, where they are helped to rejoin society.

Dr. D. is an enigma. She is a tiny Jewish woman who strikes fear into the hearts of even the most hardened addict.

"Don't mess with Dr. D.," is the word on campus.

I am repeatedly shocked at how she speaks to large men two and three times her size.

"You get down off that *blank* high horse you rode in here on, you sorry *blankety blank*! Don't think you can pull one over me! I've been around the block a few times with people like you. Your life is a piece of *blank*..."

The patients, women and men scarred by the streets of life, humbly lower their heads and say, "Yes ma'am."

The first time I attend, Dr. D. approaches me after the group and explains that she hadn't always talked like that. After a few years of trying unsuccessfully to reach the hardened patients in her groups she realized that in order to get through to these patients she has to speak their language. A language they can understand. The language of the street. They listen to her and respect her for it.

Right. Whatever works.

Sean, a member of Dr. D's group, is a black man who is part Native American. He wears his raven black hair in a thin braid down the back of his neck. He is almost twice my age, and expressed an interest in me when he found out I was Jewish. I made it clear to him, just as I did to everyone else in the hospital, that I was recovering from sexual trauma and was not interested in pursuing a relationship. Sean reassured me that his interest was in my mind not in my body. Recovering addicts are supposed to abstain during recovery anyway and he is committed to his recovery, so I have nothing to fear from him. He is a struggling Christian and I am a struggling Jewess, and so, commiserating in our spiritual doubts, we have become friends.

Sean is excited to meet a (barely) practicing Jew and has a lot of questions for me. He wants to know, as a Jew, what I think of the New Testament, and is surprised that I had never read it. He encourages me to read it so that we can discuss his questions. I explain to him that it is a huge jump for me to even consider reading the New Testament. This was not something that was allowed in my upbringing. In fact, it was unheard of.

I explain to Sean that in my sheltered world any association with Christianity was frowned upon. We were not even allowed to say the name "Jesus" in our home. Instead we said "Yushka." We didn't use the word "Christmas" either. Christmas was "Xmas," or "Chugis."

When Sean hands me a copy of the *King James Bible,* I balk. I expect to be struck by lightning at any moment. Sean gets me to agree to read it by asking a valid question. If I know the Old Testament, the Torah, to be the truth, then what do I have to be scared of the New Testament for?

He is right.

Truth is stronger than lies.

So I read the New Testament.

Sean tells me that all Christians agree that the Old Testament, the Torah, came first and was supposed to complement the New Testament. I find that hard to believe. There are so many places where the New Testament openly contradicts the Torah. Trained as I am by my Bais Yaakov education to underline and question each word in the Torah, I underlined and questioned every apparent contradiction to the Torah in the Christian bible. Sean agrees with me that something doesn't add up, but he can't explain the contradictions.

I start asking questions. I speak to the hospital priest and to ministers, but none have answered my questions satisfactorily. They all come back to the same idea. Belief in Jesus as the Messiah and the son of God takes a "leap of faith."

I have been taught that the Torah is supposed to make sense to our logical minds as well as to our souls. There is nothing I have ever encountered in the Torah or Judaism that demands blind faith without reason. I feel very spiritually aware and connected, and I desperately want to find another way to connect with God other than the way I was raised in. I am somewhat disappointed that the Christian church cannot convince me to accept Jesus. Can't they do a better job of saving my troubled soul?

Like Gabe and Adam, Sean calls me "sis" to remind me that that is how he sees our relationship and I have nothing to fear from him.

Sean is being moved to the Salvation Army, a halfway house for recovering Christian addicts. He promises to keep in touch.

My mother calls me to ask if our family rabbi, Rabbi Honigman, can come visit me. I agree. We sit in a side room off the day hall and Rabbi Honigman asks me to tell him how I'm doing. I tell him about my memories of Tatty molesting me, and that I'm trying to make sense of my life.

"I feel like a Holocaust survivor who went through the camps, and I'm asking people who were there with me: Do you remember when this and this happened? My fellow survivors, (my siblings) look at me like I'm crazy and say, There WAS NO Holocaust. It never happened. Something is very wrong with you. And you know what, Rabbi, I really hope they are right. I would rather be crazy than believe my memories. It would be easier to be insane than have my memories be true."

A few years later my father will face another accusation of child sexual abuse, this time by a male student. I will realize that Tatty is not safe around children and begin to speak out about it. Rabbi Honigman will advise my family to cut me off unless I promise never to speak publicly about my memories. He will tell anyone who asks him that I told him myself that I don't believe my own memories, and that I am not credible.

Moving again

A nurse is holding a lit match to a patient's head. She is not trying to light the patient on fire, as I first thought. She is helping her set her hair extensions. Most hair extensions are synthetic and apparently if you melt the ends together your braids will stay put. I always wanted to be a foster parent when I grew up and help traumatized children like myself. This knowledge may actually come in handy if I ever foster a black child.

I am learning that some of the staff at the hospital are just as sick as the patients. Some push drugs - selling them and giving them away for free to recovering addicts. Others are involved in sexual relationships with patients.

Some of the staff, though, are good people who truly care. An African-American nurse named Shawanda, for example, goes out of her way to help me and support me. She often tells me, "Genendy, you have to leave this place. You don't belong here. Don't become institutionalized."

She shocks me one day by presenting me with a copy of the book *Ethics of our Fathers*, with an inscription inside, "To Genendy from your nurse Shawanda." This has always been one of my favorite Jewish books. I had memorized a good portion of it in sixth grade at Bais Yaakov. *Who is rich? He who is happy with his lot. Who is wise? He who learns from everyone.*

I still can't figure out how Shawanda got hold of this book in rural nowhere U.S.A.

My copy from Shawanda is a reminder that God is indeed with me, even during my darkest moments, in one of the saddest places on earth.

It is time to listen to Shawanda. I apply to be transferred to the Elizabeth House, a halfway house run by a retired priest and sisters from the Catholic church. I have to go through a series of interviews before I am accepted. The rules at the Elizabeth House are strict. Each resident must meet with Sister Lauren for counseling once a week. We are also required to volunteer.

I am volunteering on the Oncology ward at the local hospital. It helps me count my blessings. At the front of the Elizabeth House dining room is a statue of the Virgin Mary. We pray before we eat. When it is my turn to lead the prayers, I want to pray, but my soul doesn't allow me to say the Christian prayer, so I request permission to write my own prayer.

I am granted permission.

My Prayer

All the parts of my soul
are clinging to you
crying hold me
please hold me
this is the best we can do
...the best we can do.

All the parts of my soul
are enveloped by you
still begging
hold me, please hold me
we can do nothing without you
...nothing without you.

Your spirit holds us close
we feel safe in your arms
we draw from your strength
you protect us from harm
you protect from all harm.

PART 6:

GETTING UP

"Life is like a piano. The white keys represent happiness and the black show sadness. But as you go through life's journey, remember that the black keys also create music…"
Unknown

Music

There is music surrounding me
enveloping my spirit in a
rich medley of notes
I listen to the tunes
a playful yet serious march is
nodding
for me to approach
so I come
and I hear an empty tune
listless chords aching with
loss and grief
and I cry.

Now the music is crashing and
clashing
to a furiously fast beat of anger
drumming in my ears

…Still, I listen for more
I strain
I'm beginning to hear it
almost muffled by the others
a soft tune

rising in harmony with my spirit
leaping and soaring
above all pain
beyond all fear
I connect myself to these notes
and my whole being rises
and sings along with them.

Looking for normal

I believe deep down in my soul that there must be a good reason for what I went through. In some other world, in another sphere, I know that my life must make sense. But it isn't until I enter the trauma day hospital program that I have hope that I will actually survive and maybe even heal.

The trauma day hospital program is located in the grounds of an old and established private psychiatric hospital. I begin the program while I am still living at the Elizabeth House. It is recommended to me as an alternative to what was beginning to be a habit of going inpatient so often. The program uses an eclectic array of treatments and therapies to support those recovering from the effects of severe trauma. I have weekly sessions in art therapy, movement therapy, group psychotherapy, journal writing, occupational therapy, and DBT, or Dialectical Behavioral Therapy. DBT is a method for teaching skills that helps in self-regulation and self-awareness in managing emotional trauma.

All of the adults in the trauma program were sexually abused by a parent. They all blame themselves, as I do. For us, it is a matter of survival.

Here is where I am embarking on the journey of healing the many parts of my being that have been hurt and damaged. Here I am discovering for the first time in my life, at the age of 23, that the way I relate to people isn't normal. Actually, I have no idea what normal is, as I don't know if I have ever experienced it. I don't feel part of the human race. I once had an idea that I was normal, because normal is what we are used to. Now that my world has exploded around me, I am slowly beginning to understand that my upbringing, my relationship with my parents and myself, and my traumatized brain trying to make sense of all of this, are not normal.

I also begin to understand that no one can fix me or re-parent me. I have been desperate to change the behavior of people around me, control other people's thoughts and feelings about me in order to feel safe. I always thought that if I could have more control over other people, by influencing their view of me through changing something about myself, I wasn't sure what, I could have some control. But I realize that the work is not about changing them but about changing me. I have to develop an inner nurturing parent from scratch. I have to learn to hold and validate the hurt young parts of me on my own.

This is so much easier said than done. I have so much work to do. I realize it can take years to develop and learn the skills and tools to nurture and heal myself.

I am learning that incest is unlikely to happen in families with healthy emotional boundaries. Still, it is one thing for me to understand what healthy boundaries are in theory, and completely another to be able to apply and integrate healthy boundaries in my actual life. Ideally, people learn healthy physical and emotional boundaries as babies and children through interactions with parents and caregivers. I am learning them as an adult, as rules written on a blackboard in a classroom.

I copy the ideas down in my journal:

I can say no if something feels wrong or disrespectful to me.

This is new for me. My parents taught me that they knew best and I was not allowed to disagree with them.

I can ask for what I need and want, without guilt or shame.

Really? I was not allowed to have needs. I was not allowed to have glasses.

I can have and express my own individual feelings and opinions.

Until now my parents' opinions were the only ones that were right, and the only ones that mattered. In my family, I wasn't allowed negative feelings.

In the day program, I am learning to contain the overwhelming feelings and flashbacks. Each experience, each feeling, is overwhelming by itself. I have to learn to trust myself and what I see and hear inside me. I am learning to turn down the volume using imagery and self-hypnosis. I am learning that when I am flooded with traumatic feelings and memories, I have to consciously put everything back into the disconnected compartments in my mind, and then in therapy, slowly take out one small piece at a time. It is slow, deep, painful work.

In the trauma program I explore the concept of boundaries in depth. In my religious family, the boundaries and rules around sexuality and contact with the opposite gender are unnecessarily rigid in some areas, while in other areas non-existent. For example, I remember Zaidy's anger when my ten-month-old cousin toddled into the study hall wearing only a diaper and undershirt because "modesty" had been breached. Yet I often saw Zaidy in his white boxers. And, of course, I saw him naked when he exposed himself to me in the bathroom.

I am learning that normal is simply what we are used to. This was my normal. And now it is time for me to start seeing other normals.

Strength

> *Solid strength*
> *I sense inside*
> *struggling to awaken*
> *these powers*
> *to help me cross*
> *my bridge of*
> *contradictions*
> *and reach the truth*
> *the Godliness*
> *inside me.*

Dissociation

Since learning that there is a name for what has been happening in my mind since I was a young child, I have something to work with in my healing process. I have a dissociative disorder.

Dr. Charles Whitfield writes in his book *Memory and Abuse* that dissociation is *"a defense against emotional pain, dissociation is separation from and loss of awareness of our experience of the present moment."* Repression, like dissociation is *"an automatic psychological defense against unbearable emotional pain wherein we forget a painful experience and store it in our unconscious mind."* Similarly, denial is *"a complex defense that involves not recognizing and thus avoiding our awareness of the reality of a traumatic experience. At times almost normal, denial is considered "maladaptive if it interferes with rational or appropriate action to address or heal the hurt, loss or trauma."* [1]

The only known cause of dissociative identity disorder is severe and repeated trauma in early childhood. I have all the symptoms.

So now I understand what happened to me in my family, and why my mind feels so split into pieces. I was traumatized and I dissociated and created other parts to hold the trauma. I used my creativity and made up Jay to help me cope with all of the horror. I am not the first person to do this. All of my fellow patients in the program have dissociated parts as well. We understand each other in a way that others can't. This is a known condition that results from severe and repeated trauma in early childhood. It is a real diagnosis. It can be healed. I finally make sense. I am determined to heal, although I have no concept of how many years and how much hard work it will take.

Memory

Memory is a funny thing.

---

[1] Charles L. Whitfield M.D, *Memory and Abuse: Remembering and healing the effects of trauma,* Health Communications Inc. 1993

Why would I, or anyone else, lie about something as painful and shameful as childhood sexual abuse? This is a legitimate question to ask. After all, I have no external validation for my internal truth.

I have to learn a lot about myself, and about memory, before I can make any sense of my life and of my family's view of me as a liar.

I start art therapy again at the day hospital program, and it is literally saving my life.

When I first began art therapy while in treatment with Dr. Davids, I could only express the fear, horror, pain and shame in images. I couldn't face the truth behind what was causing me to draw these pictures. My mind was protecting me (and my relationship with my family and my therapist) by blocking the memories. Then after I remembered, sometimes I retained images and other times the images disappeared, leaving just horrible feelings behind. I learned that when I dissociated during the trauma, not only did I split off and dissociate the images, I also dissociated the behaviors, the effect, and the sensations that went along with them from each other. For example, the dissociation allowed me to bite and molest my dolls as a young child, with no memory of abuse, or understanding of my behavior at the time.

Now, each time I remember again, I am in shock. I realize that I had always known, but simply didn't have the language to talk about sexual abuse. I instinctively knew my mother would never believe me if I told her. I was right about that. She doesn't believe me. According to my mother there are no monsters under the bed, and no one ever molested me.

When I tell my aunt Rivkah that I was molested by her father, my grandfather, she asks, "Where?"

"In his office," I reply.

"That's impossible," she says. "Do you remember what the door looked like?"

"No." I really don't.

"The door was transparent glass. Someone could have seen it from the dining room. If you can't remember the door how can you trust your memory of being abused?"

How can I trust my memories of being abused?

Because the door's significance paled in comparison to the experience of my trusted grandfather's fingers in my underwear.

Perhaps the glass door became entirely insignificant when it didn't protect me.

It was early in the morning, right after the morning prayers, and no one was in the dining room at the time.

I don't remember the date, or what I was wearing either.

Does that mean it didn't happen?

Does my aunt think that I *want* to remember this?

No matter what I say, my aunt and the rest of my family find a way to discount, minimize, rationalize and deny my experience.

That is what they need to do in order to survive.

This is what families of incest do, with barely a single exception.

My family cannot go to a place where they can consider the possibility of their trusted father and grandfather, their rebbe, a *talmid chacham*, molesting someone they love.

I get it. I understand denial. But it doesn't make it hurt any less.

I learn a lot of things about the workings of the mind. Long-term memory is composed of experiences that are significant to us. If an experience is not significant it does not get filed in our long-term memory.

Traumatic memory, however, has its own set of rules.

When we experience an event that feels life-threatening, all of our senses are activated. Our survival instinct, a fight or flight response, is activated.

Traumatic memories are stored in a different part of the brain than regular memory. They are stored in the part of the brain where feelings are stored along with images, and sensations they evoke. Traumatic memories are often dissociated or repressed, especially when there is no way to process them in the present. When traumatic memories cannot be processed – due to lack of validation, support or time – they cannot be filed in a meaningful context along with other long-term memories.

These unprocessed traumatic memories often come up years later as post-traumatic stress symptoms. As in my case, you can feel like the experience of trauma is happening in the moment, even if it took place 30 years earlier.

There are several famous memory studies claiming to prove that false memories can be easily implanted. I have looked at this so-called research and, although interesting, I (as well as trained trauma therapists) assert that the results do not follow through logically when dealing with memories of child sexual abuse.

I begin studying in a community college while I am in the day hospital program. I read with some annoyance about one such study in my university textbook in Psychology 101. The study involves adults who were convinced that they had been lost in a shopping mall as children. Many of them actually believed that they had been lost in a mall when, in fact, according to their parents, they hadn't been. This study lacks all understanding of what child sexual abuse feels like. Certainly, feeling lost, being lost, is a common childhood experience. But comparing being lost in a mall to being sexually violated as a child, by someone you trust and are dependent on for survival, is like comparing a distant cousin's death with a parent's death. Most children have no concept of what it feels like to be sexually violated by a trusted family member or friend. It is not an experience easily contrived or imagined, and there is nothing else quite as shameful, terrifying and mind shattering.

In another study on memory using the example of a car accident, witnesses were shown a clip of a real accident, and then asked to describe what they saw. One witness swore the car was blue, while another said it was red. One said the car slid to the right, while one said to the left. One witness believed blood was pouring from the victim's head. Another said no, it was actually coming from the victim's mouth.

While the researchers set out to prove that traumatic memory can be faulty – and indeed concluded that traumatic memory is not credible – they missed out on a crucial detail of the study. That is, not one of the witnesses claimed that they witnessed an earthquake or an armed robbery, or nothing at all. All agreed that it was a car accident. They all agreed that victims were hurt and there was blood. They accurately remembered the details that were important or shocking to them. It was only the details they considered insignificant that they forgot.

I was very young when I was abused and I will never know if every detail of what I remember is objectively accurate. But I do know that I was molested by my father and grandfather and others. I remember the experiences in the terrible ways that they affected me. Badly. I make no apologies for this, as no one in my family is willing to try to help me sort out my memories. I did the best I could to get as close to the truth as I can in my own.

Breathing, doctors, and other triggers

College is a new world for me. I was always told that college would be "dangerous," but this is nothing compared to the dangers of a state psychiatric hospital! I am 23 years old and have been in therapy for three years now. I decide that I want to study early childhood education, because on some level I realize that I need to understand the child's mind in order to understand how to heal myself. It is exciting because I am actually able to focus in a way I was never able to in high school. I am learning many things for the first time. But it is challenging because sometimes I dissociate and get distracted by my internal world of trauma and chaos. I use journaling to get through the difficult moments in class.

At college, I discover that I love to learn. The world is suddenly so big and exciting in a way it never had been, and so full of opportunity. It is wonderful. My mind is opening and developing in a way that I had not been allowed to in the restricted world of my childhood, where every secular book was suspect. I had always hated school and never did well. But I love college. I had failed biology in ninth grade, but in college I ace it. I test out of English 101 and I am placed in the honors English classes. I study writing and Japanese literature.

The teachers in community college are amazing. The honors English teacher cultivates personal relationships with each of us, even inviting us to her home for an end-of-year party. I have a social worker who helps me acclimate to my new life and manage my classes. I especially enjoy studying American history and literature. I decide to allow myself to try some activities I always wanted to try as a child but never had the opportunity to. I want to learn another language and sign up for Spanish, but I have trouble remembering the vast number of words we have to memorize. I drop out of Spanish quickly. I try piano and am not very good at it. I take ballet which is not for me, and I try yoga and swimming which are much better. I use scuba equipment for the first time during my swimming classes. I don't worry about the mixed swimming class as there is something healing about being around men in a bathing suit and not feeling like anyone is looking at me or paying any particular attention to my body. I am learning that bodies don't have to be all that scary or important. We all have bodies and we are all there to become better swimmers. It feels safe.

I am living in the city in a boarding house for women. It is in a strange neighborhood for me, downtown. This weekend I exit the house right into the gay pride parade on Main Street. Drag queens, condoms, and panty-throwing out on the street. My fellow survivors who are gay with children would never bring their kids to an event like this. My friends who are gay are just normal people trying to deal with a reality they didn't ask for, in the best way they know how. I can relate to that.

I go down to the docks with friends from the trauma disorders hospital to see the fireworks on the fourth of July. We hang out in a bar. Two peach fuzzy naval drinks - I think that's what they were called - get me drunk. My two girlfriends are kissing over my head. Gross. The whole thing is an escape from the sadness, the loss of my family, and myself. I throw up out the car window on the way home. I got drunk once before at the

Passover *Seder* when I was 15, on four cups of wine. My mother was not happy with my behavior. Neither was I, the next morning. Hangovers suck. And now I'm facing my second and hopefully last one ever. No more sweet wine.

I am sitting in our room reading a psychology textbook. Tom, the cat, is scratching in his litter box, but the sound doesn't bother me. Neither does the sound of Mary and her friends talking in the kitchen. My rented room is the only one on the first floor.

Edna Garner lived in this old mansion 100 years ago and dedicated it as a boarding home for independent women. I moved here from the Elizabeth House when I started college. Edna Garner was a woman ahead of her time. I imagine Edna Garner sitting at the piano in her long dress and tight bodice, playing a Mozart waltz. I love this house, my safe home, with its dusty old classic games and books. Edna left this beautiful old house with its grand piano, antique furniture and ten-foot ceilings to all independent women everywhere who need a place to live.

About a week before the holiday of Purim, one of my fellow residents comes to tell me someone is at the door. I wonder who it could be. I don't want to get up because I had a hard day. I am still living with the effects of the abuse every day, and I am burning with rage at Tatty. Earlier today, I sent *mishloach manos* to my younger brothers and sisters for the holiday of Purim. I made each one a separate packet with their name on it. I sent Tatty a small black water gun and labeled it "Tatty." I want to kill him or me. We can't exist together in the same universe. One of us has to go.

Earlier today, I told my psychiatrist about my feelings and he asked me if I'm seriously wanting to kill my father. I told him yes. He asked me if I have a plan. I think about my fantasy of coming home on Purim, maybe dressed as a clown with a mask, pulling out a knife and cutting off Tatty's penis as he lies on the floor drunk. Stuffing it into his mouth and strangling him with it. The fantasy is empowering. I answered the doctor honestly, "Yes, I do have a plan."

I go to the door and there is a cop standing there. "Yes, how can I help you?" I ask.

He looks at me a little confused. "Are you Genendy?"

"Yes," I smile.

"Uh... well... I'm supposed to arrest you, actually," he says apologetically. "Your doctor and therapist called you in. They are concerned that you have a plan to commit homicide."

I laugh. It just seems so ridiculous. "Yes, I did tell my doctor today that I wanted to kill my father. He molested me when I was little. I am very angry, and I do want to kill him, I'm sure you can understand that, but I won't really do it."

"Okay, I believe that," he says, shrugging. "But I'm under orders to take you in anyway. Just doing my job."

He looks at my skinny five-foot frame doubtfully and takes out a pair of handcuffs. "I have to cuff you... procedures, you know." I am not scared, just very annoyed, and mildly amused at the situation, and kind of startled for my rage to be taken so seriously. It's hard to imagine my therapist really thought I would try to kill Tatty. More likely she and my doctor are trying to set a boundary with me. Dumb idiots! Wait till I see them next. I can't wait to tell them what idiots they are.

I hold out my wrists and the officer snaps on the cuffs. He tightens them as far as he can. I slip them off and hold them out to him, smiling wryly. "Uh, they don't fit."

He scratches his head. "Do me a favor and just hold them on your hands while we walk to the car so I don't get into trouble. I don't have a smaller size, see?"

"Okay," I agree.

We walk to his car together and he asks me if I prefer to go to the station or the local hospital. "The hospital," I say quickly. "They know me in all the ones around here."

I sit in silence as we drive to the hospital. I hope I am safe and this guy won't try to assault me. I note that the doors do not open from the inside. Along the way, the officer talks non-stop about his girlfriend who left him because of his drinking problem. "I really love her and miss her. But she won't get back together until I stop drinking. And I can't do it. I tried and I just can't," he says. I empathize. I know a lot about addiction from my time in the hospital and the friends I made there. Addiction holds people in a tight grip.

We talk about addiction and I encourage the officer to try 90 meetings in 90 days, and to get a sponsor. The officer thanks me for listening to him talk, and I think about how ridiculous this whole situation is. We have to drive to another hospital as the first one we stop at is full and won't take me into the emergency room. In the hospital I am interviewed by a psychiatrist. I explain that I am very angry, but I have no intention of actually killing my father. They keep me for observation for a few hours. I get home at 2AM.

My brother Tzvi is getting married and he wants me to come to his wedding. I can't. I'm so angry. I can't face my father, my uncle Nachi, the rejection and judgments by my family. Tzvi comes to visit me and we play ping-pong. Chaya comes to visit me as well, but we don't talk about anything significant. I am enamored with my one-year-old nephew, Uriel, Chaya's second son. I am so worried about my little sister and my nieces and nephews. Could my father be abusing them? Is there any way I can get someone in my family to take me seriously? Tanta Rivka really cares. She comes to visit and I show her my art. But I feel like she can't take it in. It's too much for her to process.

Nothing happened... Nothing happened... Nothing happened...

This is the broken record my family keeps playing, a track stuck on a scratch of trauma. They simply cannot play anything else.

It's not a mystery why my family, for the most part, avoids me – and at this point, I am avoiding them too. I understand how trauma works. Trauma gets stuck inside if it doesn't get processed - stuck, just like a scratched record, playing the same few words over and over, feeling as present and traumatic as it did when it happened, even if it was 20 years ago.

We all try to run like hell to avoid traumatic memory that we can't process. We deny, repress, dissociate, rationalize, minimize. And because I can't outrun this horror – because I have to process it – my family avoids me and I avoid them.

I need to process this memory, to figure it out, and to break its hold over me and my life.

There are moments when the memories show up, sometimes unannounced. Every time I am sick, for example, and I need to go to a doctor, the following memory is triggered. Then denial kicks in:

I am about two and a half. Tatty hurt me and I'm bleeding.

I don't know exactly what he did to hurt me this time, just that he hurt me badly.

He pushed something inside me that felt like it was cutting me open, breaking me in half.

It's not the first time he did this, and it won't be the last. But it's the first time I'm bleeding like this.

Tatty takes me to the doctor.

I am terrified. I am screaming and fighting.

I do not want anyone to see what Tatty did.

It's too shameful. I know it's my fault. I'm worried that someone will tell Mommy.

I need Mommy to hold me. But I don't want her to know.

And I don't want anyone to touch me, or to look at me.

They are telling me I need help, to stop struggling, to stop moving, to cooperate.

They are trying to help me.

I don't want help. I want to die.

I want my mother.

I am not given a choice.

Adults are just stronger.

There are at least three adults here, holding me down, taking off my pants, my underwear. Holding my legs apart, looking at me, touching me. Telling me I need help, to stop moving, they will help me.

I need stitches.

It hurts when they look at me and touch me.

NONONONO!!!!!!!!!!!!!!

What are stitches?

I'm so scared and humiliated.

I don't want to have a body.

I don't want to have a bad part.

Don't tell Mommy I'm bad.

I have to get away and I can't.

I am desperate.

But I am also a tiny bit hopeful.

Maybe, they will really help me.

Maybe, they will fix me so I won't be bad anymore.

Maybe, they will get Tatty away from me and not let him hurt me anymore.

I try to bite the lady's face that is near mine. She moves her face away.

I see a needle.

My stomach hurts; I'm so scared.

Stabbing pain in one side of my vagina. I can't move. I can't get away. I feel another stab.

They are sewing me for real!

I leave in my head.

I can't be real.

I will kill off this part of me.

She is dead.

She is not real.

The real me is safe.

The real me has a Tatty who would never hurt me, and a Mommy who would know if I was really hurt, and help me.

At home, Tatty bathes me. He wants to see if I'm okay. I try to push his hand away.

NO!

He looks anyway. He always looks.

Tatty says if I tell Mommy about this he will hit me so hard I will never talk again.

I believe him.

Tatty takes me back to the doctor.

The doctor and nurse and Tatty hold me down again.

Take off my clothes again.

The doctor touches me again.

Looks at me again.

He says I'm just fine.

Good as new.

Then something I could not have guessed happens.

The doctor hurts me on purpose.

He pushes something in me down there.

His finger?

I don't know.

He is showing Tatty how to hurt me without making me bleed.

I am such a bad shameful girl.

They think it's fine to hurt me as long as I don't bleed.

I deserve it.

At home, I take a needle and stab it into my hand on purpose.

It's my way of trying to tell Mommy what happened.

Without really telling her, because Tatty said I can't.

I can't tell her anyway because

I have no words for this.

Mommy takes me to the hospital and I get stitches again.

But unlike with Tatty, Mommy is not allowed in the room.

She doesn't hold me.

She doesn't touch me when I need her.

This time I am wearing all of my clothes, strapped inside a purple straight-jacket with only my bleeding hand hanging out from where I stabbed myself with a needle.

This memory is inside me. Stuck in my mind and body. Twisting in my gut, every time I see a doctor. Every time I let a doctor touch me. Every time I see a scene in a movie with a doctor examining someone. Was it Dr. Sharp that did this? He was my pediatrician at the time. My stomach clenches, and that familiar stabbing feeling of pain, terror and shame makes the world stop for a moment.

Before I push it away, I push the memory away together with the little girl inside me who is crying.

Help me, don't hurt me.

Hold me, don't touch me.

Look at me, don't see me.

Don't tell Mommy... I need Mommy right now.

The part of my mind that was stuck in this trauma knew how to make the memory stay buried inside so I would not have to talk about it or share it. I would keep it buried by acting it out. I knew how to shame myself and hurt myself. I knew I deserved it. I didn't have a choice. Some part of me believed it would happen again sooner or later.

Now I am doing something different. Something safer for myself. For my hurt child part.

I, the adult, know the doctors in my present life won't hurt me. I know that now I DO have choices. I go to a doctor only when I can do it in a way that feels safe. I won't hurt myself anymore because of this memory. And I won't continue to doubt this little girl who thinks she is bad. I have never met a real little girl who is bad. And I know that adults molest children all the time.

I know my father molested me. I have many memories of him molesting me.

I cannot get reliable information from my family about what happened to me. They speak openly about how Dr. Sharp killed his wife, and how he was our beloved pediatrician at the time.

They speak openly about how I stabbed myself with a needle and got stitches when I was two and a half. But they cannot admit to the possibility that I was molested.

By anyone.

Ever.

Reclaiming my religion

I have a membership at the local aquarium and I often walk over there on *Shabbos*. I have my card and don't have to use money. I don't like handling money on *Shabbos*. There is a religious injunction against using money on *Shabbos*. And the truth is, I'm not so good at this "off the *derech*" thing. My soul is too connected to Torah to just let it all go. No matter how far I try to run, it is a part of me, my identity, my soul. I know in my heart that this is just a stage in my journey toward healing.

I hear the squeak of the dumbwaiter as they pull up our dinner from the basement kitchen. My nose tells me that tonight I will be eating cornbread and lasagna. Tonight I will eat dinner because it is not meat or chicken. Although I am officially off the *derech*, I still can't bring myself to eat *traif* (non-kosher meat). I don't know if I ever will. The cornbread is soft and moist, and the cheese in the lasagna melts, creamy on my tongue. When I leave the bathroom, I start to automatically recite *asher yatzar* (blessing after using the bathroom). I quickly catch myself and remind myself that I am off the *derech* and not saying blessings.

Going off the *derech* is not simple for someone with my intensely religious background. But it is necessary. I think that religion should be a physical manifestation of our spirituality. Religion should be about our connection with a Higher Power. Unfortunately, I think that many times the religion becomes more important than the connection with self and with God. That is when it begins to seem fanatical, oppressive and stupid.

In my parents' home, I always felt like religion was above protecting people's feelings, or caring about them for that matter. God came first, before people or feelings. Damn it, I get so confused. How do I know what God really cares about? I don't want to measure anything against what my family believes. I always felt separate from them. Like the real me didn't exist among them spiritually or emotionally.

To sort this out I need to separate Torah from my family, and that means I am taking a break from it.

This is easier said than done. On *Shabbos,* I hear the *lamed tes milachos* song (song about the 39 types of work that are forbidden on *Shabbos).* I taught my pre-1-A boys this song when I worked in the pre-school. The song plays over and over in my head. I know every *melacha* (forbidden work) that I am violating intimately. After all, I taught them. I can't get away from it.

And there is something else that, if I am honest with myself, I have to admit causes me crushing sadness. I miss *Shabbos*. I miss the family time, the sense of connection and belonging. As excruciating as sitting at the *Shabbos* table was, because of my misophonia, my phobia of eating and mouth noises that I struggle with since I was seven, I miss belonging to something.

I wonder if God is angry with me for needing to leave religion for a while. And then I have an epiphany: *I realize that God likely doesn't mind*. A loving God wants me to heal. A loving God wants a genuine relationship with me. God created man on Friday and only afterwards He created *Shabbos*. First man, then *Shabbos*. This proves to me that first you must be a person before you can bring religion into your life and serve God. You have to exist first in order to recognize God. Right now, I am learning to exist. I am just becoming a real person.

I share with a friend that I miss *Shabbos,* and she suggests that I contact an assistant rabbi in a nearby suburb who she knows to be open minded. We speak on the phone a few times and I explain my ambivalence about religion. Rabbi Fried listens and validates my conflict. He is warm and supportive. He assures me that there are many ways to be a religious Jew and that my family does not own the Torah or religion. He promises that his community and its culture, although Orthodox, is as different as night and day from my family.

After a few months of speaking on the phone, Rabbi Fried gently encourages me to join his congregation for the upcoming holiday of Rosh Hashana. It is an appropriate time to begin something new, he tells me. I go anxiously, and I am amazed to discover a brand-new kind of Jewish community that is diverse and open minded, as well as committed to Torah and *halakha*. One main difference between this community and my family is that culturally they are completely American. No one here is obsessed with how people dress, how much Torah they learn, and what *yichus* (well-connected family) they have. No one judges anyone else religiously. We are all on a journey to come closer to God, we are all growing and learning. We are all different. Everyone is treated with equal respect regardless of their job title, how much money they have, or their gender.

I encounter many warm and wonderful families of religious Jews who are not afraid of the real world, and are in fact an active and empowered part of it. My jeans and shorts don't bother them. The people who wouldn't dress this way assume I have my legitimate reasons. In fact, one of my new friends takes off his black hat when he sees me because he knows the sight of it makes me queasy. The Torah is not his hat. He is not his hat.

This community is diverse. All the way from black hat and wig to shorts and no hair covering. Some of the members don't look so Jewish on the outside, but the prayers they say, the Torah they read, the *Shabbos* they keep, is the same one I am familiar with. It is a perfect bridge for me between two worlds and I am so grateful to have found somewhere I can belong spiritually.

Coming back

She stands in shul on Shabbos
for the first time in years
facing the open ark
doors spread wide
like angels' wings
the people and the room
slowly disappear

all that remain are the ark and the
voices
the ark and praying voices.

She is a little girl standing in her
grandfather's yeshiva
watching from the doorway of the
women's section
because she isn't allowed in
the people and the yeshiva slowly
disappear
all that remain are the ark
and voices
the ark and
screaming voices.

The Torah watches in horror
the Torah hears in sorrow
the little girl's silent protest
as her grandfather
the rosh yeshiva
takes her into
the bathroom and undresses
as the bochurim
sneak her upstairs and
tear her soul to pieces
the Torah sees it all.

Then the yeshiva is ripped down
nothing remains but a mound of

crushed wood
and piles of torn holy books
cascading down broken stairs
the Torah is shipped away
her memories buried in its parchment...

...This week in shul again miles and years away
she sees the Torah and remembers
what it witnessed
she is so very angry
why did you stand by and watch what was done to me?
why didn't you help me?

The Torah answers
It was I –
the same Torah who
lives in this shul today
I was there in that yeshiva
from the time you were born
and I saw it all
I bear witness
I've been waiting for you
Wrap yourself in me and I'll hold you.

On Rosh Hashana, the *Aron Kodesh*, the ark, is opened and the sight of the Torah within brings tears to my eyes. This Torah is identical to the Torah that I remember seeing in Zaidy's *yeshiva*. Only now things are so different. Now I am permitted to touch the Torah, to hold it, and even dance with it on the festival of *Simchat Torah*. I challenge Rabbi Fried about that.

"I thought that a woman can't touch a Torah scroll because she is impure." I question Rabbi Fried constantly because so much that had been forbidden to me is now fair game. I want to understand and make sure it is legitimate.

"A Torah scroll does not absorb impurities," the rabbi explains. "And in any case both men and women are considered ritually impure until the arrival of the Messiah when we will all be purified." I knew my family would consider it scandalous for a woman to dance with the Torah, but I am one woman who is clear that I must hold and dance with the Torah in order to reclaim it. In order to heal our relationship.

Finding love

Several families invite me back for *Shabbos* week after week and soon I find myself spending almost every *Shabbos* and holiday with my new community. On one of these weekends, a young couple ask if they could introduce me to a friend of theirs, a man named Yossie. I am 24 years old, still in the trauma disorders day hospital program, and I do not feel ready to date. My friends assure me that there is no pressure. Yossie is not told that the *Shabbos* meal is a set-up. He is simply invited for *Shabbos,* so I am encouraged to observe him from a safe distance, with no commitments.

In spite of myself, I am attracted to this blond, blue-eyed introvert, with the glaring inability to hide his feelings. I can see almost immediately that Yossie is very different from my family. Yossie expresses an interest in dating me and we go out for Chinese food that Saturday night. Soon we begin dating almost every weekend. I am slowly getting to know Yossie. There is no guessing with Yossie. If he is upset or angry, he and I both know. If he is happy or excited, he and I know that too. Yossie is honest to a fault, and so refreshingly real. He grew up completely secular, in a world I have never known and have no relationship with. He is introducing me to a side of America I have never experienced before, pro football, jazz – Miles Davis, Coltrane and the Blues Brothers. He is smart and talented in a way that I cannot relate to, and driven and stubborn in a way that I can. Yossie is an artist and a musician, prone to depression when he is not being creative, complex and moody, caring, and fiercely loyal. I like him a lot.

Yossie wants to propose after three weeks of dating, and I am shocked. I explain that I would have to date any man at least a year before I could even consider marriage. I tell him I had some bad experiences with men in the past and I have trust issues.

"Lots of girls have issues with men," Yossie says calmly. "I've dated and supported a lot of them. I'm cool with that."

"You don't understand..." I really don't know what to say. I don't want to put him off, but I am not ready to explain the extent of my issues.

"What don't I understand?" he asks gently. "I want to understand."

Yossie asks me a lot about my family, enamored that I had grown up religious with so many siblings. It gives me an idea.

"You like the idea of marrying someone who comes from a large religious family... which is something you don't have, right?"

"Well, yeah, that is attractive. My family is completely secular."

"Well, you won't be getting a religious family if you marry me. You won't be getting any family. You will just be getting me. My family and I are estranged."

He looks concerned. Good.

"Why?"

"It's a long story. I'm not sure I'm ready to share it yet. We only met three weeks ago. I will tell you, though, that I have serious issues, and that I am actively working on them, and that I'm not ready to get married. You should get to know me better before you think about marriage...We just started dating. I don't want to lead you on, but I didn't think this would be an issue because I understood that guys coming from the secular world expect to date for a long time…"

Yossie looks at me. "That's usually true," he says, "but this is different."

"Why?"

His blue eyes hold mine for a long moment. This is getting scary.

"Because I'm sure you're the one." This is more than scary. This is dangerous. I have to push him back. And fast.

"Listen. I'll tell you exactly what's wrong with me. My father and grandfather sexually abused me when I was very young. My family don't believe it happened and say I'm a liar and I'm nuts. I've tried to commit suicide and I've been in a mental hospital, and as a result of the abuse I have a dissociative disorder."

"What's that?"

"Ever heard of Sybil?"

"Whoa, hang on, you have what Sybil had? You have multiple personalities?"

"Not by definition. It used to be called multiple personality disorder because it can look that way. But now we know that people who have this disorder are really just one person who dissociates. I'm not as dissociated as Sybil was. I don't lose time or do things I'm not aware of. But I do have dissociated parts. I made them up to survive. It's a condition that kids who are exposed to severe and repeated trauma in early childhood sometimes develop. It happens in the stage of imaginary friends. I made up some imaginary friends to help me because there was no one in my real world who could."

"How many parts do you have?"

"I don't know, maybe five or six? I'm not sure."

Yossie looks at me with furrowed brows. I can feel my arms trembling. Does he think I'm nuts? If I were Yossie, I would run for the hills.

"Is dissociation like schizophrenia?"

"No, it's completely different. Schizophrenia is a psychosis and is biologically based. Dissociative disorders are a coping mechanism, a reaction to severe trauma, and are environmentally caused."

"Do you really believe these parts are separate people?" he asks.

"No, because they aren't. I know they are all parts of me. But at times they do feel very separate. Sometimes when I'm alone, scared or stressed I switch and I let them come out and take over. You wouldn't necessarily notice. It's part of what I had to do to survive. I had to believe that the abuse was happening to some other person, in some other world. I couldn't have survived and grown up otherwise. It worked for me then, but now it's not functional anymore. Parts of my head are stuck in the traumatic past and I will probably be in therapy for a long time, trying to heal and integrate my mind."

There, I am telling him the truth. I am letting him know that my mind is broken. If that doesn't scare him away, then nothing will.

Yossie gazes at me with a serious, thoughtful expression. He strokes his short reddish-blond beard. "I'll have to think about this," he says.

I can breathe again. Yossi is gone.

Or, I thought Yossie was gone, but I underestimate Yossie. The next time we speak, he has everything worked out. "I read some books and talked to a psychologist. I think you'll be in therapy for another couple of years, and then you'll be fine," he says with confidence. "I can handle this dissociation thing."

"But I won't push you," he adds. "If you need to date me for a year, I can wait. Take your time."

The lack of pressure is a relief.

A week later, after three months of dating, I tell Yossie that I am ready for him to propose. He proposes that weekend in *shul* in front of the *Aron Kodesh*, the Holy Ark, with a beautiful ring with a setting of diamonds, and inlaid, a sapphire. Of course, I say yes. Yossie and I are thrilled. We know that neither of us is perfect but we believe that we are perfect for each other.

Our engagement is a time of joy, anticipation, anxiety - and lots of arguments. Our backgrounds are as different as night and day, and we are learning a new language, one that helps us understand each other despite our vast cultural differences.

I am very concerned about the impending wedding and the physical intimacy marriage entails. Although I am interested in the idea of physical intimacy, the reality of actually allowing myself, or anyone else, that close to me, potentially reminding me of the ways that I was hurt as a child, the fear, anger and betrayal, is frightening. Will I be able to do it? Will I be able to separate sexual abuse from marital intimacy? I'm not sure. Yossie is less concerned. He says we will work through whatever comes up together. He promises that we will go to couples' therapy if we need to.

We meet with Yossi's rabbi and his wife to express concern about the sheer number of arguments we are having. The rabbi's wife gives us a valuable tool that we will use for many years and arguments to come. There are three rules to a good fight, she says. The first is no blaming, the second is no name-calling, and the third is no bringing up past issues. If you follow these three rules your fights will be productive and healthy and you can argue as much as you want to. We would continue to argue.

One thing we don't argue about is religion. Yossie became religious four years earlier and I recently started keeping *Shabbos* again. I explain to Yossie that I don't know if I will ever be able to completely resolve my issues with Judaism, and I am not even sure what I believe right now about the Torah. In the meantime, I tell him that I am willing to commit to keeping the "three biggies" - *Shabbos*, kosher, and the laws of "family purity." Yossie also asks me if I would agree to wear a hat on my head, as is the custom of married Orthodox women, when I leave the house, and I agree that I will.

Chaya, always the family spokesperson, informs me before the wedding that if my father is not invited to the wedding and also given an honor at the wedding, no one in the family will come. I feel like my arm is being twisted, but I want my family there, so I agree. I plan to give my father the honor of reciting one of the seven blessings during *bentching* (prayer after the meal). Our family custom is for each set of parents to walk their own child down the aisle. I can't stand the thought of Tatty touching me, so I ask Yossie if he would be willing to follow the Hassidic custom and have both fathers walk him down the aisle and both mothers accompany me. Yossie has his own feelings of animosity toward my father for what he did to me, but he agrees to sacrifice his comfort for my sake.

Eight months after we get engaged, we are tying the knot in a Chinese restaurant, minus the Chinese food. (The chicken and rice are excellent, though.) About 100 people attend. We have two bands that are taking turns playing. A Jewish band, friends of mine who play during the ceremony, and a jazz band, friends of Yossie, who play during the reception.

My entire family attends the wedding, and I am glad they are here, but it is strained and awkward. (It is the last time I will see some of them for many years). I am nervous and my throat hurts. I hope I won't give anyone strep when I kiss them. I want to stay centered, grounded, and focus internally. I am holding the younger parts of me close. Before the ceremony, I pray that God embrace me in light and love and joy. I ask God to help me breathe and relax and be in the moment. And I ask God to please hold me and Yossie close because there is no way we will be able to build a successful marriage without His help. I feel grateful, and a sense of wonder and disbelief. Is this really ME getting married?!

Getting married seems like the end of one chapter and the beginning of another. It is a moment in which perhaps I move on from painful family relationships and start a whole new healthy relationship of my own. But creating a healthy relationship after years of incest, isolation and gas-lighting is not as simple as it sounds. The process of rebuilding my life and my identity is its own painful and joyful tale, the subject of my next book.

FAST FORWARD

"Broken glass still glitters in the sun."
Tara Martinez

The year is 2018, almost 20 years after Yossie and I celebrated our marriage in the Chinese restaurant. As far as I know my parents are alive and well. My father is set to retire from his job as a school principal this year. About 19 years ago my father was investigated for allegations of child sexual abuse by a male student. He was not prosecuted for lack of sufficient evidence. I have heard personally from two former students of my father that he molested them as well. Neither is yet willing to make their allegations public.

About four years ago I started a blog with the hope that I could prevent more children from being abused by my father. I have tried to reach out to my mother and siblings on a few occasions and they have made it quite clear that they are not interested in a relationship. Although I am alone now, I never lose hope that someday at least part of my large family will find healing and reconciliation.

I have been living in Israel for the past 12 years with Yossie and our three children. We live in a community very similar to the one I grew up in. I have been in therapy for years, and I am at peace internally with my past, with the loss of my family, and with the mission that I have accepted to help educate and heal others from the scourge of child sexual abuse. The dissociated parts that protected me as a child have been integrated. I am an activist, and in past years I helped found and run a child safety organization in my community. I was the subject of a recent documentary depicting how we as a community are working from within to prevent and heal the problem of child sexual abuse and incest.

I am grounded, safe, and connected to myself, my husband and children, and my community. I have been blessed with the miracle of healing.

Every morning I pray to be a source of healing, hope, light, love and strength to others who are still struggling with sexual trauma, as I did.

One survivor who reached out to me a few years ago, a young mother with five small children, is the granddaughter of a famous Hassidic rebbe. We are constantly amazed at how much we have in common. No, her father and grandfather did not molest her as mine did. She was a victim of severe emotional and physical abuse by her mother, and of incest by a brother. Both of our grandfathers are now in the world of truth, and we both have the firm conviction that they are supporting us from the other side, begging us even, to speak our truth and heal ourselves, our families and our communities. If we learn one thing from our holy Torah, from Moses and King David, to King David's daughter Tamar, who publicized the rape by her brother Amnon, it is that our leaders' greatest mistakes are not be hidden or glossed over, but laid out clearly for us to discuss, learn from, understand and repair.

I sit in front of a class of 25 precious little girls, five and six years old. I have been teaching pre-school for over 20 years now. Today I am talking to my students about boundaries as they have been playing doctor in school lately. It is normal for young children to be curious and explore their bodies by playing doctor. But this is a good opportunity to teach them about personal safety.

We are studying *shuls* this year in my classroom, and we have already visited three. My students are all religious and have all been to *shul* many times with their families. They know that a Torah scroll is holy, and when not being read from is always covered with a special decorated covering. I tell my girls that their bodies are precious, holy and private, just like a Torah scroll. I point out that we are covered with clothing for this reason just like a Torah. Our pet dog, who often accompanies me to work, doesn't wear clothes because his body is not holy and private like ours. His body does not contain a *neshama* (holy soul) like a person's body. I explain that just like we don't uncover a Torah scroll without a good reason, we also don't uncover our private parts without a good reason.

One little girl raises her hand.

"Taking a bath is a good reason."

"Right," I say. "What might other good reasons be?"

Another voice pipes up, "Using the bathroom is a good reason. And a doctor can check us with our mommy right there."

"That's right, because visiting a doctor is a good reason. But *playing* doctor is *not* a good reason to take your clothes off. And no one, not even parents or a doctor, can touch private parts without a good reason. Private parts are the parts of your body that are covered with a bathing suit."

The girls have a lot to say about this topic. One little girl shares that her neighbor, the same age, asked her to take her clothes off and she said no, and told her mother right away. We praise her for doing exactly the right thing.

I tell the girls that, sadly, some older kids, and even adults who we might know and like, may not know these important safety rules. If they ever meet someone like that, someone who asks them to undress or wants to touch them in private places, they should tell a trusted adult right away because it is not okay for anyone to do that to them.

I share a true story about a real little girl, a child who was in my class last year, whose uncle, a man who she loved, and usually liked to play and read with, wanted to touch her private parts one day as part of a game. She felt scared. She knew in her heart that her body was private and holy, but she thought her uncle knew that too. She was very mixed up. She didn't protest because she didn't want her uncle to stop playing with her. The little girl was scared to tell her mother. Maybe her mother would be angry with her for playing this game with her uncle?

My students watch me with wide eyes. I ask them, "Well, what do you think she should do? Should she keep it a secret?" A chorus of adamant nos. A few scattered yesses.

"Well, guess what happened? The girl told her mother even though she was scared to, and her mother wasn't even a little angry with her! In fact, she gave her a prize for being so brave and telling her the truth. She told the girl that it is the adults' job to keep children safe, and it is her mother's job to make sure that her uncle stops."

"Because you know," I continue, "it is never a child's fault if a big kid or an adult is mixed up about these safety rules. And it is not your job to say no to an adult. That's why it's so important to tell another adult if something like this happens, so they can protect you."

A little hand is up. "Yes?"

"One time my friend hit me here," she points to her backside, "and I didn't like it."

"Your friend made a mistake," I say. "No one is allowed to touch your body in a way that makes you feel uncomfortable. It's good that you are telling us about it. In our class we respect each other's bodies and privacy. And if someone makes a mistake we talk about it and help them fix it."

I take these precious, innocent children into my heart each year, and I know that I am doing what I can to educate and protect them. I also know that for some of these girls my little talk won't be enough. Some of them will be abused anyway, and some will tell, and some won't. (eighty percent of children do not tell.) I pray for a world where we don't need to worry about such things as incest and child sexual abuse, and where we don't need to tell such scary stories to young children. I pray for a world that is loving and safe for every child and adult.

And I believe that it is happening as I write this. I believe that together we are making it happen.

GLOSSARY

Aron kodesh	The Holy Ark where the Torah scroll is kept in synagogues and study halls
Asher yatzar	The blessing made after going to the bathroom
Ba'al Shem Tov	18th century Jewish mystical rabbi considered the founder of Hassidic Judaism
Bais medrish	Study hall
Bar mitzvah	Coming-of-age ceremony for 13-year-old boys
Bas mitzvah	Coming-of-age ceremony for 12-year-old girls
Bekishe	Long black silk coat worn by Hassidic men
Bentching	Blessing after meals
B'nos	Girls' group
Bochur/Bochurim (pl)	Young unmarried men or adolescent boys studying in yeshiva
Boro Park	Neighborhood in Brooklyn, New York with large ultra-Orthodox community
Bris	Circumcision
Chas v'shalom	Heaven forbid
Chashuv	Important
Chillul Hashem	Disgrace of God's name
Chizuk	Strength
Cohen	Priest
Chametz	Leavened food
Chumros	Stringencies
Chuppah	Canopy beneath which Jewish marriage ceremony is performed
Dayan	Religious judge

Davening	Praying
Derech	The "path" or the way of God
Erev Pesach	The eve of Passover
Frum	Religiously observant
Gadol hador	The great man of the generation
Gedolim	The "Greats," meaning the great rabbis
Goyish	Gentile-like
Halakha/ halacha	Jewish law
Hassid	A Jew who practices a form of Judaism called Hassidism or Hassidic Judaism
Hassidic/Hassidish	A Jewish school founded in the 18th century by the Ba'al Shem Tov in Europe, which practices mysticism, devotion, seclusion, and strict adherence, among other things. Researchers estimate that there are currently 400,000 Hassidic Jews practicing around the world
Kinderlach	Children
Kohen	Priest
Litvish	A Jewish school of ultra-Orthodoxy, also founded in 18th century Europe, which stands in opposition to Hassidic Judaism. Its focus is more rationalistic, less emotional-devotional, and in some areas stricter than Hassidic Judaism. The feud between these two schools characterized ultra-Orthodox Jewry for much of its history, even until today.
Lamed tes milachos	The 39 primary prohibitions for work on the Sabbath
Melacha	One of the 39 primary prohibitions for work on the Sabbath
Mah nishtana	The four questions recited at the Passover Seder
Mein Tochter	My daughter

Mishloach manos	Gifts of food sent to family and friends at Purim
Mitzvos	Commandments from the Torah
Mohel	The man whose duty is to perform the ritual circumcision on a baby
Mussar	Religious morality
Negiya	Literally "touch," or the prohibition against boys and girls or men and women touching in any way
Neshama	Soul
Pesach	Passover
Peyos	Sidecurls worn by ultra-Orthodox men and boys
Pikuach nefesh	A matter of life or death
Rav/ Rabbi/ Rebbe	Religious leader
Rebbetzin	The wife of a rabbi
Rosh yeshiva	The head of the yeshiva, the religious school
Savta	Grandmother
Seder	The Passover ritual meal
Sefarim	Books
Shabbos	The Sabbath
Shacharis	The morning prayer
Shaila	Religious query for a rabbi
Shidduch/shidduchim (pl)	Marriage prospect. Set-up for a (sometimes) arranged marriage
Shirayim	Leftovers from the rebbe's table
Shiva	Seven-day ritual mourning practice upon the death of a close relative
Shnell	Quickly
Shtreimel	Fur hat worn by married Hassidic Jewish men
Shul	Synagogue
Sukkos	Holiday of Tabernacles
Talmud chacham	Great scholar

Talmidim	Students
Tanta	Aunt
Tatty	Daddy
Tish	Table, the rebbe's table, where Hassidic men flock for lessons, singing and rituals
Traif	Not kosher
Tzanua	Modest dress
Tzitzis	Ritual fringes
Tzniut	The practice of keeping the laws of modest dress
Yeshiva	Religious school
Yetzer hara	Evil inclination
Yichus	Family lineage
Yiddishkeit	Judaism
Zaidy	Grandfather